EVERY HC
EVERY MAN A WARRIOR

*Stories of the Forts and Men
in the Upper Ohio Valley During the
American Revolutionary War*

Michael Edward Nogay

Copyright © 2009 by
Michael Edward Nogay
P.O. Box 3095, Weirton, WV 26062
All Rights Reserved

ISBN: 978-0-578-01862-1

Printed by Tri-State Publishing Co., Steubenville, Ohio

Front Cover Art © John Buxton. Used with permission

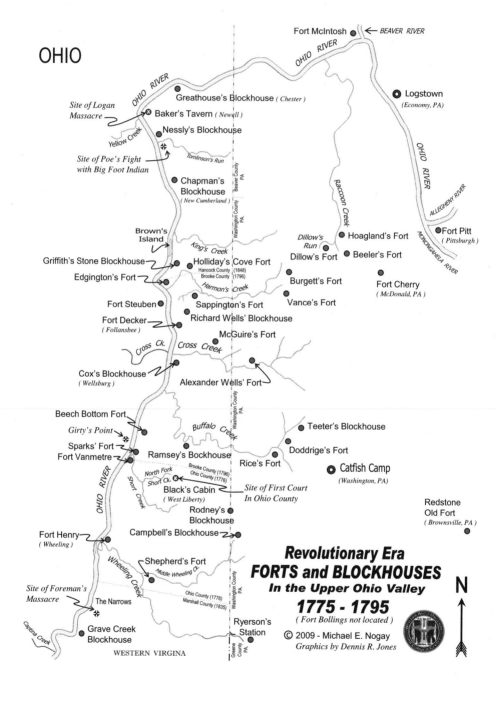

OHIO

Fort McIntosh ← *BEAVER RIVER*

OHIO RIVER

OHIO RIVER

Greathouse's Blockhouse (*Chester*)

◉ Logstown
(*Economy, PA*)

Site of Logan Massacre — ◉ Baker's Tavern (*Newell*)

Nessly's Blockhouse

OHIO RIVER

ALLEGHENY RIVER

Yellow Creek

✳

Tomlinson's Run

Site of Poe's Fight with Big Foot Indian →

Chapman's Blockhouse
(*New Cumberland*)

Beaver County PA

Washington County PA

Raccoon Creek

Brown's Island

King's Creek

Dillow's Run ● Hoagland's Fort

Fort Pitt
(*Pittsburgh*)

Griffith's Stone Blockhouse —

Holliday's Cove Fort
Hancock County (1848)
Brooke County (1796)

Dillow's Fort ● Beeler's Fort

MONONGAHELA RIVER

Edgington's Fort —

Harmon's Creek

Burgett's Fort

Fort Cherry
(*McDonald, PA*)

Fort Steuben ●

Sappington's Fort

Vance's Fort

Fort Decker —
(*Follansbee*)

Richard Wells' Blockhouse

McGuire's Fort

Cross Ck. *Cross Creek*

Cox's Blockhouse —
(*Wellsburg*)

Alexander Wells' Fort —

Beech Bottom Fort

Girty's Point →✳

Teeter's Blockhouse

Buffalo Creek

Sparks' Fort —
Fort Vanmetre —

Ramsey's Bockhouse
Brooke County (1796)
Ohio County (1776)

Doddrige's Fort

Rice's Fort

Washington County PA

North Fork
Short Ck. ⊗

Catfish Camp
(*Washington, PA*)

Black's Cabin
(*West Liberty*)

Site of First Court In Ohio County

Rodney's Blockhouse

Redstone
Old Fort
(*Brownsville, PA*) ●

Fort Henry —
(*Wheeling*)

Campbell's Blockhouse —

OHIO RIVER

Short Creek

Shepherd's Fort

Wheeling Creek
Middle Wheeling Ck.

Site of Foreman's Massacre →

The Narrows

Ohio County (1776)
Marshall County (1835)

Washington County PA

**Revolutionary Era
FORTS and BLOCKHOUSES
In the Upper Ohio Valley
1775 - 1795**
(*Fort Bollings not located*)

N

✳

Captina Creek

Grave Creek
Blockhouse

WESTERN VIRGINIA

Ryerson's Station

Greene County PA

© 2009 - Michael E. Nogay
Graphics by Dennis R. Jones

TABLE OF CONTENTS

AN UNBROKEN WILDERNESS

"Our whole country is in forts."
--June 8, 1774 letter from Col. William Crawford to General
George Washington

The *History of the Pan-Handle* was published in Wheeling in 1879. Edited by J.H. Newton, it is considered the most complete, if somewhat dated, writing on early Hancock, Brooke, Ohio and Marshall counties, in what is now the Northern Panhandle of West Virginia. Newton described the Ohio Valley of the late 1700s vividly:

> At that time the country was an unbroken wilderness – the haunt of wild beasts and savages. Every home was a fort, and every man a warrior. [1]

White settlers began migrating to the Ohio Valley in significant numbers following the end of the French and Indian War in 1763, despite a royal proclamation forbidding them from settling west of the Appalachians. With them, they brought a burning desire for land, but also diseases like smallpox, as well as a hunger that consumed the natural resources of the river valley.

There were three substantial Indian tribes in the Upper Ohio Valley at this time: the Shawnee, the Delaware, and the Mingo. [2] The Delaware had originally been know as the Lenni Lenape and occupied land on the Delaware River in Eastern Pennsylvania. The Delaware tribe kept the new name given to them by the settlers even as they were forced to move westward towards the Ohio.

The Iroquois Nation was comprised of six tribes located largely in upstate New York. Each of these tribes was divided into clans with a "clan mother" exercising considerable tribal authority, unusual in a masculine society.

The Shawnee had once occupied what is now the state of West Virginia and Western Pennsylvania until they, too, were forced by white migration to move to lands northwest of Fort Pitt and the Ohio River. The Shawnee had the greatest numbers among these tribes, with their main encampment in what is now Chartiers, near Pittsburgh. [3] The tribe lived on land which would soon be claimed by no less a speculator than the great George Washington.

Across the mighty Ohio, the ferocity of the Wyandot Indians was unchallenged. By 1774, the Shawnee and other tribes were ready to put an end to the pale intrusion, and the frontiersmen prepared for the onslaught.

> The atmosphere at Wheeling in the spring of 1774 was warlike. This frontier town ... was filled with crowds of expectant migrants ... all touched with Kentucky fever and anxious to be the first to find the fertile locations in the promised land. [4]

Fort Pitt was the flagship in the fleet of forts and blockhouses that would spring up throughout the Ohio Valley to protect these settlers. Its position at the headwaters of the Ohio, where the Monongahela converged with the Allegheny, meant that all migration by water travel into the Ohio Valley started there.

The fort at the great confluence had been in the hands of the French in the mid-1700s, when it was called Fort Duquesne, until the French and Indian War ended. In 1770, John Murray, the colonial governor of New York who bore the title Earl of Dunmore, had been sent to govern Virginia. Fort Pitt was renamed Fort Dunmore for a short time in honor of the new governor by a young doctor*, John Connolly, who commanded it for a short while for the British. Connolly was soon taken prisoner by the colonists in 1775 after Lord Dunmore fled the country. The Americans in Pittsburgh and the Ohio Valley thereafter exercised "home rule" for the first time. The taste of self-governance is one that became habit-forming for the frontiersmen.

The French and Indian War had been a complex conflict between the French and the British, each with their allied Indian tribes fighting for control of the St. Lawrence and Ohio River valleys. The British called it the Seven Years' War.

---

*It has been questioned whether Dr. Connolly actually completed his medical studies. See, Gary S. Williams, *Spies, Scoundrels and Rogues on the Ohio Frontier* (Baltimore: 2005) 23.

As that war came to an end with the Treaty of Paris in 1763, Scotch-Irish and other European immigrants began pushing through the Allegheny and Appalachian mountains, seeking to settle the river valley below the confluence, while fleeing religious intolerance and dreadful harvests abroad.

The French ceded control of the frontier to the British and the crown sought to appease the Indians with a "proclamation" outlawing further westward migration. The royal decree set no precise boundary but sought to establish a line between "civilization" and the "savages." It was swiftly ignored, allowing the colonists to realize they could defy the King from across the Atlantic with little fear of reprisal. Rather, the governments of the colonies of both Virginia and Pennsylvania sought to stake claims to Pittsburgh and the new settlements along the Ohio River.

The great Daniel Boone came overland, making him the first white settler through the Cumberland Gap in 1767 and later one of the first permanent settlers in the bountiful hunting grounds of "Kantuck-kee." A bit further north, Ebenezer Zane went west through the forest* from Old Fort Redstone (Brownsville, Pa.) and reached the Ohio River at a place called "Weiling" by the Indians. Twenty miles upriver, John Holliday and Harmon Greathouse arrived at a cove on the Ohio and founded a settlement in 1771 named after the former, on a creek named after the latter, and which today is known as Weirton, West Virginia. The genie could not be put back in the bottle; more settlers would soon follow.

The University of Pittsburgh published *Council Fires on the Upper Ohio* in 1940. Its author, Randolph C. Downes, believed that in September of 1775, with the Virginia militia occupying Ft. Pitt, "Americans thus had control of the situation in the Ohio valley..."[5]

The native Indians had other ideas.

Although the fighting strength of the Mingo Indians in 1777 was limited, "their power was greatly increased by the alliance with them of half the Shawnee nation, some Delaware and a few scattered

---

*One historian claims Zane and his family made the trip from "the South Branch via Redstone Fort from which they floated down the Monongahela and the Ohio in canoes and pirogues." J. M. Callahan, *Semi-Centennial History of West Virginia* (Charleston: 1913) 25.

Wyandot." In the spring of that year, a "mixed band of Mingo, Shawnee, Delaware and Wyandot... besieged Wheeling ... and other stations, burned supplies and carried off the horses, in order to prevent the raising of crops and to force the pioneers to abandon the country." [6]

Despite the fact that the Shawnee, Wyandot, and Delaware Indian tribes dominated the Ohio Valley, European demand for beaver hats and deerskin jackets brought white fur traders to the valley, their lust for profits outweighing concerns for personal safety. With them the traders carried guns, powder and lead, which the Indians coveted. The iron axes and knives were beyond the ability of the Indians to produce, and the only currency they had to acquire such tools were furs and skins. For even the white settlers, "furs constituted the 'people's money.' They had nothing else to give in exchange for rifles, salt, and iron on the other side of the mountain." [7]

As Professor James B. Whisker has noted:

There are many firsthand reports available to us that show that the Indians gave up their traditional weapons soon after they came into contact with firearms...[one Indian chief said] 'After I saw the first rifles...I did not rest until I owned one...I gave my bow away forever...We could make arrows for our bows, but we could not make powder and lead for our guns...but I would not lay aside my gun.' [8]

The frontier maintained, at times, an unsteady peace, always on the edge of calamity, a shaky truce made possible only by the bridges built through trade.

Over-hunting and trapping became the norm. Christian missionaries reported Delaware warriors each shooting up to 150 deer per year. One trader once purchased 23 horse loads of pelts from the Indians in an area northwest of Ft. Pitt. Due to their dense fur, beaver pelts were in high demand in Europe. The results were devastating. In the mid-1800s Pennsylvania still held abundant herds of elk, wolves and mountain lions; but the beaver had all but disappeared.

As the game populations dwindled and the white population rose, Indians were forced to range further westward on their hunting expeditions. At the time the basic diet of the Ohio Valley tribes consisted of food from two sources: "hunting provided the protein and farming the carbohydrates."

> [An Indian] village of 200 adults and 200 children would require 300 pounds of meat each day. A deer would yield between 40 and 50 pounds of meat, and the village would need six to eight deer each day...[9]

Living on the meat of non-domesticated animals came at a huge price. The Indians became reliant upon the white traders to repair their muskets and refill their powder horns in order to be able to supply such vast amounts of game.

The liberal supply of the white man's hard liquor wreaked havoc on Indian society. The amount of alcohol sold and traded to the Indians was staggering. As early as 1772, records indicate the Gratz brothers sold "two hogsheads" (470 gallons) of liquor to a merchant for resale to the Indians. By 1779, over 17,500 gallons of rum were traded to "less than a thousand Delaware and Shawnee warriors, about 17 and a half gallons per warrior." Not surprisingly, even that sobering figure pales next to the rum consumption by the colonists: nearly 4 million gallons of the intoxicant in 1772 alone. [10]

On March 24, 1777, a Council of War was held at Ft. Pitt by the settlers in response to the growing Indian threat of reprisal. It was determined that Col. William Crawford should "station twenty-five men, (each) at Logstown (Economy, PA in Beaver County), Holliday's Cove (Weirton, WV) and Cox's (Wellsburg, WV) upon the Ohio." [11]

Already established a year earlier, Holliday's Blockhouse-- soon to become a fort-- was Western Virginia's first line of defense along the Ohio. In fact, later that year, on August 17, 1777, Major Henry Taylor marched his men from Reardon's Station on Raccoon Creek to "take the minds of the people" after Indians in the area had raised an alarm. The mindset of the settlers at Holliday's Cove Fort was to stay and fight.

Wrote Maj. Taylor:

> The inhabitants of Holliday's Cove declared they would stay and defend themselves as long as they could and secured

all the ammunition and guns, telling me that they would account with the public for all they would use of them. [12]

Col. Crawford, who would later be burned at the stake, wrote to Congress on April 22, 1777, that Indians had killed and scalped a man at nearby Raccoon Creek below Ft. Pitt two weeks earlier and had tomahawked another victim at Wheeling. [13]

Unfortunately, the worst was yet to come.

CHAPTER I

CAPTAIN SAMUEL MASON:
THE CRIMINAL COMMANDER

Fort Henry in Wheeling is best known for the courage of its inhabitants and militia in the face of Indian attacks under the command of Col. David Shepherd. As a literate man among an illiterate population, his numerous letters to his commanding officers at Ft. Pitt memorialize Shepherd's role as a leader of the Ohio County, Virginia* militia on the frontier. However, another commander of that militia unit had a much more notorious side. Walt Disney even made a movie based in part on Samuel Mason's life, the 1955 classic *Davy Crockett and the River Pirates*. Even the History Channel noted his "survival at Ft. Henry on August 31" on its "This Day in History" segment.

Samuel Mason (1739-1803) (sometimes referred to as "Meason") was part of the Ohio Valley's military hierarchy. He was known for having survived the first siege of Fort Henry in 1777, despite being wounded. In January of that year, Mason was appointed a captain in the Ohio County, Virginia, militia. [1] Within six months of his appointment at Ft. Henry, Mason sought to ingratiate himself with the commander at Ft. Pitt, writing to Brig. Gen. Edward Hand:

> I set off at eight this morning and flatter myself that you will not disapprove our proceeding, but call on me, if any

---

*Ohio County, at the time of the Revolutionary War, encompassed the entire Northern Panhandle of what is now West Virginia. It was formed in 1776 from Virginia's West Augusta District.

occasion should require, and as I may not return to the ensuing council at CATFISH (Washington, PA), I take this opportunity of returning to you the strength of my company, which consists of fifty men, furnished for going on any emergency.

In the late summer of 1777, Ft. Henry was attacked by Indians. Earlier that season, Lt. David Shepherd had allowed nine companies of soldiers to return to their homes, and by the last day of August only two companies remained in the fort, those of Capts. Joseph Ogle and Samuel Mason.

On the morning of September 1, 1777, Mason marched 14 men out of Ft. Henry against what he thought was a force of six Indians. Soon Captain Mason and his men were intercepted by the Indians and nearly all literally cut to pieces. [2]

Twice wounded, Mason concealed himself by the side of a large fallen tree. Captain Ogle and his 12 scouts sought to aid Mason's company, but were likewise struck down. Of the 26 enlisted men in the hostilities, 23 were killed and two seriously wounded. Curiously, Captain Mason survived by hiding himself in the bushes until nightfall, while the enlisted men under his command died in battle. [3]

Mason's true character began to reveal itself further when he was charged in court in a "Recognisance." On April 1, 1778, court records reveal that Mason was accused and convicted of the first documented case of public corruption in Ohio County. A hero at Ft. Henry only months earlier, Mason was fined "five pounds and an equally good gun" for having exchanged his own property for a better weapon from the Continental Stores at Ft. Henry. [4]

Captain Samuel Mason was described by George Edgington in an 1845 interview as having a "singularly Roman hook nose, only equaled by (that of) his son John's...he settled early on Wheeling Creek with a bad name from the start."[5]

The collection of the great 19th Century historian, Dr. Lyman Draper, contains a receipt dated April 27, 1778, indicating Mason was still a commander in Wheeling at that time. It reads: "Received fourteen flints of Zephaniah Blackford for the use of my company. Given (under) my hand, Samuel Mason, Captain."

The notes of Dr. Draper also contain several other hints regarding the character of Captain Mason. A soldier named Captain Samuel Murphy told Draper that, years before his Ft. Henry service, Mason had stolen horses in Frederick County, Virginia, and was "pursued, overtaken and wounded and the horses recovered." Mason did not limit his treachery to wealthy victims, however.

In a Draper interview with Colonel G.W. Servier, Mason is accused of an even more revolting offense: he and his cohorts were "charged with stealing from Negro cabins on Sabbath days when their occupants were attending church; and articles were found in their possession." Possibly a more vulnerable class of victims has never existed in this country.

As his Revolutionary War service drew to a close, Mason last served as a militia captain in Ohio County in May of 1781, as reflected in his recorded attendance at a "Courts Martial." During these later years, Mason resided "two miles east of Wheeling and kept a tavern there in 1780." [6]   It was normal for militiamen to have a full-time trade outside the army, but Mason was now ready to embark on a more treacherous occupation.

Mason is said to have moved about this time to nearby Washington County. A "Samuel Mason" is listed as living in Donegal Township, Washington County, Pennsylvania, according to a *Listing of Inhabitants in 1781 in Washington County, Pennsylvania*, published by Shirley G.M. Iscrupe and the Southwest Pennsylvania Genealogical Service in 1991.

In a recent book, Mason is described as follows:

Mason was a man of gigantic size and minuscule conscience. He killed for both pleasure and profit, but had not always been a lawless man. Mason had been an officer in the army during the Revolutionary War and had served with distinction. He was promoted to Captain and was twice cited for bravery. [7]

Another historian has Mason relocating to Kentucky in 1781 to claim lands he had been granted by Congress for his revolutionary service. Dr. Draper's notes include a letter written by Mrs. William Anthony, the daughter of Captain John Dunn. Mrs. Anthony claimed that while in Kentucky, Samuel Mason terrorized her father when he refused to cooperate with Mason in a counterfeiting scheme. After beating Dunn to near death, Mason and his gang later ambushed and murdered Captain Dunn on an early, cold morning near Henderson, Kentucky.

Mrs. Anthony, apparently to revenge her father's death, chronicled the criminal pursuits of Captain Mason. [8]

Mason eventually moved south seventy miles down the Ohio to Illinois where he took control of a tavern and inn near a notorious outlaw hideout called Cave-in-Rock. There Mason began plying the trade of river pirate. Using women to lure unsuspecting cargo boats to shore, Mason and his partners, the Harpe brothers, Micajar (Big Harpe) and Wiley (Little Harpe) (who was yet known by a third name, John Setton), would ruthlessly murder the crews and seize their goods. Authorities eventually drove out Mason and his gang. [9]

Moving next to the Mississippi River, Mason became even more daring. He is said to have "amassed a fortune" over the next five years through thievery, while settling on the old Natchez Trace, an Indian trail between Natchez, Mississippi and Nashville, Tennessee.

John L. Swaney had been a mail carrier along the Natchez Trace around 1796. He later told J.C. Guild, the author of *Old Times in Tennessee*, that he knew Mason and his gang. Swaney said that Mason and his men committed one of their most infamous robberies upon Colonel Joshua Baker of Kentucky.

The September 14, 1801, edition of the *Kentucky Gazette*, reported that Col. Baker and his companions were robbed of "their horses, traveling utensils, and about two thousand three hundred dollars." When Baker subsequently sought to apprehend Mason, the bandits threatened Col. Baker not to continue his efforts to recover his money, and "the pursuit of the robbers was abandoned."

Nonetheless, Samuel Mason's son, John, "a mere lad," was soon arrested in Natchez and convicted of the robbery. He was sentenced to receive the punishment of 39 lashes and exposure in the pillory.

After receiving each "blow of the cowhide which tore the flesh from (his) quivering limbs," John Mason shrieked the same despairing cry of "innocent, innocent." At the conclusion of the flogging, young Mason shaved his head, stripped himself naked, mounted his horse, and "yelling like (an) Indian, rode through and out of the town."

Weeks later, Samuel Mason confronted one of his son's jurors, who is said to have wanted the boy hanged. After threatening the juror with a tomahawk and rifle and forcing him to pray to his Maker, Samuel Mason, "regarding him with a bitter smile, swore his life was not worth taking, wheeled around and in an instant disappeared." [10]

When the United States purchased the Louisiana Territory from France, the new federal authorities sought to eliminate criminal activity along the Mississippi. Authorities soon offered a $2,000 reward for Mason's capture, dead or alive.

In 1804, seeking to take over Mason's gang and earn a huge bounty in the process, "Little" Wiley Harpe and another gang member, James May, came up with a plan to murder Mason. After burying a tomahawk in Mason's brain, the two men severed his head and took it to the seat of the territorial government of Mississippi to collect their reward.

In a strange twist, Rothert wrote that, earlier, in 1799, "the head of Big Harpe had been placed on the end of a pole," by vigilantes some 20 miles south of Cave-In-Rock, at a place still called "Harpe's Head."

Little Harpe's plan for the reward was foiled, however, when he and May were recognized as bandits themselves. They were hanged at a place known as "Gallows Field," where their heads too were placed on poles. Their headless corpses were buried along the Natchez Trace, the very highway they had terrorized. The Mason gang's exploits had come to an end.

The news that Samuel Mason had at last been killed was a great relief to the country. The fact that Little Harpe and James May were actually hanged was a matter of equally widespread interest. [11]

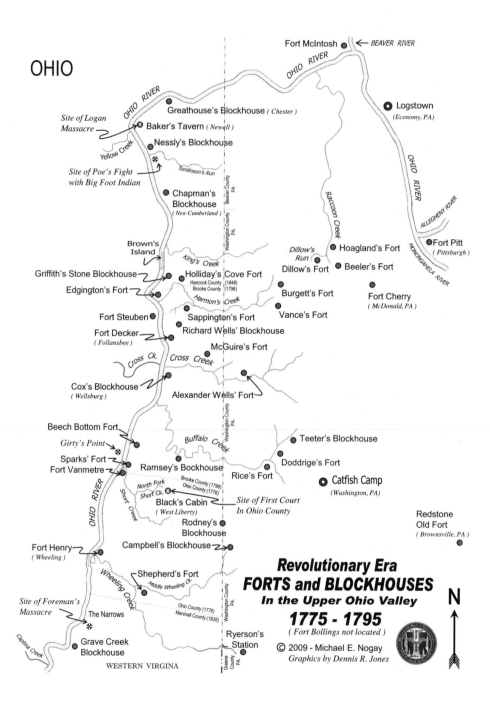

OHIO

Fort McIntosh ● ⟨⟨ ← *BEAVER RIVER*

OHIO RIVER

Greathouse's Blockhouse (*Chester*)

● Logstown
(*Economy, PA*)

OHIO RIVER

Site of Logan Massacre

⊗ Baker's Tavern (*Newell*)

● Nessly's Blockhouse

Yellow Creek

Site of Poe's Fight with Big Foot Indian

Tomlinson's Run

OHIO RIVER

ALLEGHENY RIVER

● Chapman's Blockhouse
(*New Cumberland*)

Beaver County PA

Washington County PA

Raccoon Creek

Brown's Island

Dillow's Run

● Hoagland's Fort

● Fort Pitt
(*Pittsburgh*)

MONONGAHELA RIVER

King's Creek

Griffith's Stone Blockhouse

Holliday's Cove Fort
Hancock County (1848)
Brooke County (1796)

Dillow's Fort ● Beeler's Fort

Edgington's Fort

Harmon's Creek

● Burgett's Fort

Fort Cherry
(*McDonald, PA*)

Fort Steuben ●

Sappington's Fort

Vance's Fort

Fort Decker
(*Follansbee*)

Richard Wells' Blockhouse

McGuire's Fort

Cross Ck. *Cross Creek*

Cox's Blockhouse
(*Wellsburg*)

Alexander Wells' Fort

Washington County PA

Beech Bottom Fort

Buffalo Creek

● Teeter's Blockhouse

Girty's Point

Sparks' Fort
Fort Vanmetre

Ramsey's Bockhouse

● Doddrige's Fort

North Fork
Brooke County (1796)
Ohio County (1776)
Short Ck. ⊗

Rice's Fort

● Catfish Camp
(*Washington, PA*)

Short Creek

Black's Cabin
(*West Liberty*)

Site of First Court In Ohio County

Redstone
Old Fort
(*Brownsville, PA*)
●

Rodney's Blockhouse ●

OHIO RIVER

Fort Henry
(*Wheeling*)

Campbell's Blockhouse

Wheeling Creek

Shepherd's Fort
Middle Wheeling Ck.

**Revolutionary Era
FORTS and BLOCKHOUSES**
In the Upper Ohio Valley

N

Site of Foreman's Massacre

The Narrows

Ohio County (1776)
Marshall County (1835)

Washington County PA

1775 - 1795

Capina Creek

Ryerson's Station

Grave Creek Blockhouse

Greene County PA

(*Fort Bollings not located*)

© 2009 - Michael E. Nogay
Graphics by Dennis R. Jones

WESTERN VIRGINA

- 12 -

CHAPTER II

THE MURDERS AT BAKER'S TAVERN

On April 30, 1774, a mass murder that attracted worldwide attention occurred at Baker's Tavern, across the Ohio from the mouth of Yellow Creek near the present-day site of Mountaineer Race Track and Casino, in Hancock County, West Virginia.

The murder of Chief Logan's brother, nephew, pregnant sister, and possibly his wife, sparked Lord Dunmore's War as well as an outpouring of international sympathy and the outrage of future president Thomas Jefferson. The incident was also the genesis of perhaps the most eloquent speech ever delivered by a victim of injustice.

R.G. Thwaites and L.P. Kellogg published *The Documentary History of Dunmore's War, 1774* in 1905. The book is a compilation from the Draper Manuscripts. The witness affidavits published therein make it clear that the massacre of Logan's relatives at Baker's Tavern was perpetrated by a "party of whites called Greathouse's party," along the Ohio River on the Virginia side opposite Yellow Creek.

The affidavits are somewhat disjointed, as each witness seemed to recall the incident differently. However, certain common themes emerge, and therein lies the truth of what actually transpired that spring day.

Thwaites called Joshua Baker's establishment on the Ohio River "a low grog-shop tavern," and indicated Baker had "recently been warned not to sell more liquor to the Indians," a short time before the killings. [1]

George Edgington, son of Holliday's Cove hero Thomas Edgington, was interviewed by the famous historian Dr. Lyman Draper in 1845. His recollection was that a party of Indians from

> ... the town fork of Yellow Creek ... stopped at Baker's, drank. Mrs. Baker told Daniel Greathouse that a squaw

told her (in a drunken fit) that the Indians intended to murder Baker's family before leaving. Greathouse went and raised a party of about 30 men ... there an Indian (Logan's brother) was drinking and strutting around in a military coat, someone shot him and (Edward) King then stabbed him while in the agonies of death, saying "Many a deer have I served in this way."

Edgington recounted that another Indian warrior and two women "were shot by Daniel Greathouse and John Sappington. One of the squaws had a child that was saved and sent to Col. [John] Gibson [who was purported to be] its father. Twelve Indians were killed in all. Greathouse died of measles the following year." [2]

Draper also interviewed several others about the Baker's Tavern murders. The founding father of Steubenville, Ohio, Bezaleel Wells*, told Draper in 1845 that Greathouse and his party believed that

[Col.] Michael Cresap's party had killed an Indian at the mouth of Capteen** the day before the affairs at Baker's ... (and) Greathouse and his party, thinking the war had now broke out, concealed themselves and engaged Baker to get the Indians drunk – one of whom got drunk, took down a military coat and put it on, swaggering around swearing "I am a white man," when John Sappington shot him... Greathouse's party ... then killed others in camp, Logan's sister, etc. [3]

Judge Henry Jolly, who was 16 years old in 1774, later told Draper that Greathouse's party got most of the Indians drunk at Baker's Tavern and then challenged the sober Indians to a shooting contest. When their guns were emptied, the white men tomahawked

---

*Bezaleel Wells, who later became a Jefferson County Probate Judge, and his partner, James Ross, purchased 3538.5 acres on October 24, 1796, at the newly-opened Federal Land Office in Steubenville, Ohio. Wells is said to have plotted the "first legal settlement in the Seven Ranges; he named it Steubenville, after Fort Steuben." See Edward T. Herald's, *The Founding of Steubenville*, 1796-1802 (1948) 23-24.

** Captina Creek, a tributary to the Ohio located just below Grave Creek Blockhouse near present-day Moundsville, West Virginia. See map herein.

and "shot them down; the [Indian] woman attempted to escape by flight (and) was also shot down. She lived long enough to beg mercy for her baby, who she said had been fathered by Col. John Gibson who had been a trader amongst the Indians." Jolly indicated that Cresap's men were not present at Baker's Tavern, but did command a party of whites that later overtook the surviving Indians who were escaping down the Ohio, a few miles past Grave Creek. Cresap's men attacked the Indians, and thus "the first overt acts of [Dunmore's] War have usually been attributed to Michael Cresap..." [4]

Michael Cresap, Jr., son of Col. Cresap, would later tell Draper that the massacre of Logan's family began over a coat. Cresap, Jr., had been told by Joseph Tomlinson that

> Indians went into Baker's [Tavern] and without permission took liquor and drank and also took what rifles there were and put on Nathaniel Tomlinson's military coat.

After Tomlinson told the Indian to remove his regimental coat, Daniel Greathouse, John Sappington, and Nathaniel Tomlinson killed the Indian when he refused. Cresap, Jr., indicates he was told that George Cox, seeing what was about to transpire, left Baker's and "had not gone far in the woods [when he] heard firing at the house... Baker (also) had no hand in it." [5]

Cresap, Jr.'s account of the incident vindicates his father, Col. Michael Cresap, whom Chief Logan blamed for the murders.

In his *Chronicles of Border Warfare* (Clarksburg: 1831), A.S. Withers wrote a largely apologetic account of the Baker's Tavern murders. Of interest, however, is his footnote that discusses Col. Cresap's killing of the Indians south on the Ohio at Captina Creek, that by other accounts occurred earlier that week:

> Col. Andrew (Van) Swearingen*, a Presbyterian gentleman of much respectability... says the disturbance opposite Yellow Creek preceded the engagement at Captina and that

---

*Col. Van Swearingen was the militia commander of Holliday's Cove Fort in 1777 who led men in a large canoe down the Ohio in the middle of the night in aid of Ft. Henry which was under attack by the Indians.

the latter, as was then generally understood, was caused by the conduct of the Indians, who had been at Yellow Creek and were descending the river, exasperated at the murder of their friends at Baker's.

Ruben G. Thwaites, the successor to Dr. Draper at the Wisconsin Historical Society, added a footnote to the revised edition of Withers' work in 1895:

Withers is altogether too lenient in his treatment of the whites engaged in this wretched massacre.

Chief Logan (whose Indian name was Talgahyeetah), was born around 1725, the son of a Cayugo Indian of the Iroquois League of the Six Nations. Logan was not married at the time of the incident at Baker's Tavern according to most accounts and thus it would not have been possible for his "wife" to have been a victim as several books suggest. It is clear that Logan's sister was murdered, however. J.A. Caldwell wrote in 1880 that Logan's "sister was the wife of General John Gibson, then an Indian trader, and the mother of the child who was spared at the massacre at Bakers..." [6]

In his famous speech, known by rhetoricians as "Logan's Lament," and subsequently recited by school children around the country, Logan blamed Colonel Cresap for the murder of his relatives. The speech was said to have been spoken by Logan to his brother-in law, Col. John Gibson, who was the "sole listener" and its subsequent translator:

I appeal to any white man to say if he ever entered Logan's cabin hungry, and he gave him not meat; if he ever came cold and naked and he clothed him not. During the course of the last long and bloody war, Logan remained idle in his cabin, an advocate for peace.

Such was my love for the whites, that my countrymen pointed as I passed, and said, "Logan is a friend of the white man." I have even thought to live with you but for the injuries of one man, Colonel Cresap, who last spring in cold blood and unprovoked, murdered all the relatives of Logan, not even sparing his wife and children.

There runs not a drop of my blood in any living creature. This has called me on for revenge. I have sought it; I have killed many; I have fully glutted my vengeance. For my country, I rejoice in the beams of peace. But do not harbor a thought that mine is the joy of fear. Logan never felt fear. He will not turn on his heel to save his life. Who is there to mourn for Logan? Not one. [7]

This grieving speech of Logan was published in 1775 by the Virginia *Gazette* and caused a worldwide stir. Thomas Jefferson, the future president of the United States, took a particular interest in the notorious affair at Baker's Tavern and published Logan's words in his *Notes on Virginia*. Thereafter, Jefferson's version of the speech was published in the famed McGuffey *Reader,* and became a favorite school recitation piece.

Logan yet again blamed Cresap in a note he dictated a few months after the murders. After taking a man by the name of Robinson and others hostage, in retaliation for the Baker's Tavern murders, Logan forced Robinson to pen the following note for him:

Captain Cresap:

Why did you kill my people on Yellow Creek for? The white people killed my kin at Conestoga a great while ago, and I thought nothing of that, but you killed my kin again on Yellow Creek and took my cousin prisoner. Then I thought I must kill too; and I have three times since the war: but the Indians are not mad, only myself.

- Captain John Logan

After massacring another family by the name of Holston, Logan left the note tied to a war-club at the scene. It was found a few days later. Brant and Fuller believed in 1891 that the note by Logan charged Captain Cresap, the son, and not Col. Cresap, the father, with the murders at Baker's Tavern. [8]

Such spurious arguments have clouded the truth behind the Logan murders over the years.

To his *Notes on Virginia* originally published in 1785, Thomas Jefferson wrote an amended appendix titled "Relative to the Murder of Logan's Family." Jefferson incorrectly stated that "Col. Cresap, a man infamous for the many murders he had committed on these much-injured people," commanded a party which had ambushed and killed "the family of Logan, which had long been distinguished as a friend of the whites" in the spring of 1774.

Jefferson also erroneously wrote that the massacre occurred on the Kanawha River (several hundred miles south), rather than the Ohio River, and compounded his error by placing the Baker's Tavern murders at the hands of Cresap.

In 1797, Maryland Attorney General Luther Martin, who just happened to be Col. Michael Cresap's son-in-law, published a letter claiming the speech of Logan and the accusations against Cresap were both fabrications. It was later asserted by at least one historian that after Jefferson's death, the late president had a letter in his possession from Gen. George Rogers Clark, exculpating Cresap and blaming Greathouse but that Jefferson never published the same. [9]

Martin sought to defend the name of his wife's family. He attacked Jefferson's publication of Logan's speech and wrote in the Philadelphia *Gazette*:

> I am convinced the charge exhibited by him [Jefferson] against Colonel Cresap is not founded in truth; and also, that no such specimen of Indian anatomy was ever exhibited... in the death of Logan's family Colonel Cresap, or any of his family, had no share. [10]

On December 31, 1797, Jefferson wrote a rebuttal letter to Governor Henry of Maryland, apparently because his critic, Martin, was a Maryland state officer. Jefferson complained that Martin had never brought his concerns directly to him before publishing his letter in the Philadelphia newspaper, as protocol would have dictated. Jefferson defended his inclusion of Logan's speech in his *Notes on Virginia*, as follows:

I copied, verbatim, the narrative I had taken down in 1774... I knew nothing of the Cresaps and could not possibly have a motive to do them an injury with design.

Jefferson complained that 23 years had passed since the killings at Baker's Tavern, and few witnesses still survived. Jefferson contacted General John Gibson who was still living and who "had been the translator of the speech." Gibson confirmed to Jefferson that

...the speech of Logan (was) genuine... [but, wrote Jefferson] if it shall appear on inquiry that Logan has been wrong in charging Cresap with the murder of his family, I will do justice to the memory of Cresap... If, on the other hand, I find that Logan was right in his charge, I will vindicate... the truth of a chief, whose talents and misfortunes have attached to him the respect and commiseration of the world. [11]

A letter dated February 4, 1800, from Fort Henry's esteemed Col. Ebenezer Zane to a Kentucky senator also vindicated Cresap. Although Captain Cresap had killed "the Indians" on a canoe on Captina Creek 40 miles south of Baker's Tavern in April, 1774, Zane wrote that

I must do the memory of Captain Cresap justice to say that I do not believe that he was present at the killing of the Indians on Yellow Creek [Baker's Tavern].

Zane goes on to write that "there can scarcely be doubt" that the murders at Baker's Tavern and the subsequent killing of Indians by Cresap's party on the Ohio "were the cause of the war immediately following, commonly called Dunmore's War." [12]

However, A.S. Withers in his *Chronicles of Border Warfare* (Cincinnati: 1895), writes that "Dunmore, as royal governor of Virginia, had several reasons for bringing matters [between the Indians and settlers] to a head - - he was largely interested in land speculation under Virginia patents," which would be worthless in the event Pennsylvania troops took control of Fort Pitt, then garrisoned by Virginia militia. Dunmore, wrote Withers, "favored a distraction in the shape of a popular Indian war."

James Chambers swore, in an affidavit given on April 20, 1778, that "in the spring of the year 1774, (he) resided on the frontier near Baker's Bottom [Tavern] on the Ohio…" Chambers stated that Daniel Greathouse and Edward King solicited him to go to Baker's to kill Indians who were encamped on Yellow Creek after they were "made drunk by Baker," and after learning Michael Cresap had earlier killed some Indians on "Grave Creek," which is opposite Captina Creek on the Ohio. Chambers stated that Greathouse and King and their party killed and scalped the Indians present at Baker's Tavern, "except a little girl." [13]

John Jeremiah Jones published a defense of Cresap in 1826 titled *A Biographical Sketch of the Life of the Late Colonel Michael Cresap*. A revised version of the book was republished by Otis K. Rice, who wrote in a forward that Jones,

> …undertook the writing…for the purpose of disproving the charge of the Mingo chief, Logan, that Cresap had murdered Logan's family [and was thus] responsible for the conflict known as Dunmore's War [but decried Jones' book as] filled with flaws and deficiencies.

The greatest contemporary historian of the Ohio Valley for the revolutionary period, Alan W. Eckert, clearly believed that Daniel and Jacob Greathouse, along with Edward King and Joseph Tomlinson, had perpetrated the Logan family murders at Baker's. Eckert wrote that Michael Cresap had participated in the killing of three Indians a week earlier at the mouth of Captina Creek, but had resisted the urgings of Jacob Greathouse to murder Logan's family who were camped on Yellow Creek.

Eckert maintains that the Greathouse party of 26 men killed seven warriors at Baker's including Logan's older brother, Taylanee [known also as John Petty] and his nephew, Molnah. Also murdered were Logan's "wife," Mellana, and his pregnant sister, Koontay, though Eckert in an endnote admits some authorities indicate Logan was unmarried. Eckert does believe a little girl was spared and eventually was given to her father, John Gibson, to raise.

Eckert maintained that a group of warriors, upon hearing the initial exchange of gunfire, crossed the Ohio at Yellow Creek in canoes to aid Taylanee, Logan's brother. Of this second group, 12 Indians were murdered, bringing the death toll to 21 at Baker's Tavern. [14]

Eckert believed that John Gibson, to whom Logan had delivered his famous speech, later told his brother-in-law that Cresap had *not* been involved in the Baker's Tavern affair. By this time, however, the speech had been delivered to Lord Dunmore, and it was not changed. [15]

Tales concerning the Logan Massacre continue to evolve to the present day. An otherwise insightful book, *Choosing Sides on the Frontier in the American Revolution* published in 2007, strangely maintained that in January 1772 it was William Crawford who had "slaughtered Logan's family," causing Indian retaliation on the frontier. There is absolutely no evidence to support such a claim or date.

In a 2008 book about Daniel Boone, Meredith Mason Brown writes that "a white man named Greathouse" who had killed several relatives of Chief Logan on Yellow Creek 17 years earlier, was attacked in March, 1791, on the banks of the Ohio, near Limestone, Kentucky. The Indians:

> … seized Greathouse's flatboat as it came down the river, according to the captain of another flatboat that had passed Greathouse's boat and that itself was attacked. Greathouse and his group were roaring drunk. Simon Kenton and others found the naked body of a big man, Greathouse, lying by a sapling with (his) intestines wrapped around the trunk. The Indians had cut the intestines of Greathouse… tied the severed end to the sapling and forced (him) to walk around the sapling, winding (his) intestines around it until (he) died. The manner of Greathouse's death may have been a coincidence, but it smacks of a payback for the killing of Logan's sister. [16]

Brown does not state which Greathouse, Jacob or Daniel, is supposed to have met this tortured end. George Edgington told Dr.

Draper in 1845 that Daniel had died of measles in the year following the 1774 massacre. [17] Eckert writes that it was Jacob Greathouse and his wife who endured this grisly fate at the hands of Shawnee Indians in Kentucky, who had recognized the perpetrator of the murders at Baker's Tavern. [18]

The murders of Logan's family sparked a war and hundreds of years of international debate by some of our nation's greatest thinkers. Sadly, however, it is memorialized today by the State of West Virginia with only a small roadside historical marker near the intersection of WV Routes 30 and 8 in Hancock County, several miles from the site of the actual incident on the banks of the Ohio River.

CHAPTER III

"FORTING UP"

Dr. Joseph Doddridge, in his classic 1824 book on the Ohio Valley during the American Revolutionary period, writes of families "belonging" to a fort, much like one today would belong to a church. ("The fort to which my father belonged was … three-quarters of a mile from our home.") Doddridge recollects how, as a little boy, a gentle tapping on the door with the whisper of the word "Indian" would cause entire families to abandon their homes and flee to the neighborhood fort. [1]

As Dr. Doddridge noted about the Ohio River frontier:

A well-grown boy, at the age of twelve or thirteen years, was furnished with a small rifle and shot pouch. He then became a fort soldier and had his port hole assigned to him. Hunting squirrels, turkeys and raccoons soon made him an expert in the use of his gun. [2]

In other ways, however, the Ohio Valley frontiersmen quickly adopted the institutions of the genteel folk back east. Justice was meted out in jury trials as early as 1773. The following year, Presbyterian missionaries were giving "many of the early settlers in Western Pennsylvania the first taste of formal religion they had had since they left their old homes." German Catholics had settled in nearby Westmoreland County, Pennsylvania by 1787, and Irish Catholics had built St. Patrick's Sugar Creek Church by 1805. All told at the time, only "one-sixth of the entire population of western Pennsylvania during the pioneer period was church goers."

One author called the Ohio Valley of the late 1700s "the frontier of the unchurched." Ministers who tried to convert these souls were called "circuit riders" as they took the Bible to the people, conducting services, weddings and funerals, sometimes in exchange for food and lodging.

> Circuits usually followed the streams where most settlers built their cabins, running from the mouth to the headwaters on one side and back down the other... If the circuit rider found a young man with the proper spirit who showed some ability for public speaking, the preacher recommended him for the position of "exhorter," which meant that he could serve as the local minister until the circuit rider returned on his next round. [3]

One of the unsung historians of the Ohio Valley during the Revolution was a Presbyterian minister named John Dabney Shane (1812-1864). In the early 1840s, as the last of the original settlers of the river valley were entering their twilight years, Shane collected their oral histories in written notes, an unusual technique for the era. In *Border Life* by Elizabeth A. Perkins, Shane's work is compared to that of the great Dr. Lyman Draper, who outlived Shane and purchased his historical collection at Shane's estate auction. According to Perkins:

> ...John Shane crisscrossed the Ohio Valley countryside, recording interviews and conversations with more than three hundred informants on backcountry life...Shane immersed himself in the vanishing cultural world of the Ohio valley settlers through two decades of intensive research... Shane labored to save their humble stories for posterity at a time when Founding Fathers and Revolutionary War heroes strode more confidently across the pages of history. [4]

As a cleric, Shane was obviously interested in the religious beliefs of the men and women he interviewed. Writing mostly of those who had settled in Kentucky, and in the Lower Ohio Valley, Shane also preserved histories of Indian attacks and the "random brutality of frontier life." One of Shane's interviewees told just how dangerous it was to go out at night on the frontier: "most settlers barred their doors and stayed inside from sunset to sunrise."[5]

But even in those times, life still took on a sense of normalcy. According to J.A. Caldwell:

> The first occasion on which the gospel was preached on Wheeling Creek…was in the summer of 1772. The minister was David Jones of New Jersey who made missions to the Indians in 1772 and 1773 on the west side of the Ohio.

Dr. (Rev.) Joseph Doddridge performed the first marriage ceremony in the newly-organized Brooke County, Virginia on June 1, 1797, uniting Dabby Brown and Robert Walker in marriage.[6]

Three Springs Church was constructed in northern Ohio County (now Hancock County) in 1790 on land donated by James Campbell. It was built of logs and was the "mother" church of the Cove and Paris (Pennsylvania) United Presbyterian churches. Three Springs Cemetery is located on a main thoroughfare of the same name in present-day Weirton, West Virginia, just off Cove Road Hill. The cemetery is the final resting place of several of Holliday Cove's earliest settlers and is now owned and maintained by the Hancock County Commission. [7]

The first service preached at Three Springs Church near Holliday's Cove was by Rev. John Brice, who came up from Stone Church at the forks of Wheeling Creek escorted by four armed men who provided protection from the Indians. The renowned Presbyterian revivalist and preacher, Elisha McCurdy, according to a West Virginia historical maker near the site, served as the first pastor of Three Springs Church in 1799. Five years later, the church was relocated to the top of Cove Road Hill. A monument in nearby Frankfort Springs, Pennsylvania, at the junction of Old Route 22 and Pa. Route 30, just below Raccoon Creek, memorializes this great orator.

Virginia and Pennsylvania had long been at odds over which colony would control the Ohio Valley. A group of land speculators from Pennsylvania, led by Thomas Wharton of Philadelphia had proposed a scheme in 1772 to create a new colony named "Vandalia." It would have encompassed much of what is now the state of West Virginia. Although the British Privy Council had recommended its adoption, the Vandalia scheme failed when it was strongly opposed by Virginia land owners. Even today the highest honor bestowed by West Virginia University is the "Order of Vandalia."

In 1773 Pennsylvania established Westmoreland County which encompassed the area of Fort Pitt, in what is now Allegheny County. Its seat of government was located at Hannastown, about three miles northeast of Greensburg. At the time of its destruction by Indians on July 13, 1782, Hannastown contained about 30 log houses which surrounded the tavern of Robert Hanna. [8]

The Virginians countered with the establishment of West Augusta District. Eventually, the boundary dispute between the two states was settled when surveyors laid out the Mason-Dixon line.

The Acts of the Virginia Assembly in October 1776 divided the District of West Augusta into three new counties: Ohio, Yohogania and Monongalia.

The first court in Ohio County was held at Black's Cabin (also known as "Courthouse Fort") on the north fork of Short Creek in present-day West Liberty on January 6, 1777. David Shepherd, who was to command Ft. Henry, was named a justice of the peace. Samuel McCulloch, who would soon make his famous "leap" over Wheeling Hill to avoid capture by the Indians, acted as surety for his brother, John, who was appointed High Sheriff of Ohio County. [9]

On June 2, 1777, Shepherd took his oath and was appointed a colonel of the Ohio County militia; Sam McCulloch was sworn in at the rank of major. The Ohio County Court eventually moved its bench and bar to Wheeling, with the last session held at Black's Cabin in 1797. [10]

Indian raids on settlers occurred most often in the spring and summer months, rather than when the Ohio Valley Indians were wintering elsewhere. These raids were often encouraged or even directed by the British, who, by the late 1770s, were engaged in brutal combat back east with the revolting Americans. A fort consisting of blockhouses and stockades made of heavy logs was a formidable barrier to native Indians who did not have artillery. The local militia was essentially volunteer, and the men themselves popularly elected a captain or colonel. Public embarrassment was the only punishment for a militiaman who refused to serve or returned home. [11]

As Charles A. Wingeter correctly noted in his 1912 book, *History of Greater Wheeling and Vicinity:*

> The settlers who served in the garrisons at Fort Henry, or Grave Creek, or other points along the Ohio, were not only a home guard defending their family and property, but were in reality soldiers of the Revolution, repelling an attack directed by England against the new national cause.

Indian attacks were still feared on the Ohio River as late as 1794. On January 11 of that year, the first regular packet line between Pittsburgh and Cincinnati was formed. The passengers on these boats, according to the advertisements, would be offered "Protection from Indians."

> No danger may be apprehended from the enemy, and every person will be under cover made (bullet) proof to rifle ball, and convenient portholes for firing out. Each of the boats is armed with muskets and amply supplied with ammunition, strongly manned with choice men and the master of approved knowledge. [12]

By present-day standards, such an honest disclosure of the perils involved in passage on the Ohio would seem to have frightened away more customers than it attracted.

In his 1924 well-documented text on Ohio River piracy, Otto A. Rothert, noted that for many pioneers traveling the Ohio on flatboats in 1795, Indians were not the only concern.

> ... pioneers floating down the Ohio or Mississippi on flatboats came in contact with comparatively few savages,

but were exposed to a far more daring and dangerous enemy in the form of river pirates – white men, many of them descendants of supposedly civilized European families. [13]

One of the most treacherous of these river pirates was none other than a militia captain who was a hero in the first siege of Ft. Henry, Samuel Mason.

Pittsburgh served as the primary point of embarkation for immigrants moving down the Ohio River. Water-driven sawmills in the area of Ft. Pitt ripped lumber for flat-bottomed boats, commonly measuring 50 to 100 feet in length and 15 to 25 feet in width. Other pioneers came by land and crossed the Ohio by ferry. In late 1789, Absalom Martin received the first license from the territorial governor to operate a ferry across from Wheeling. The site was appropriately known as "Martins Ferry," Ohio. [14]

By 1796, Ebenezer Zane had convinced Congress to allow him to extend a wagon road, known as Zane's Trace, from Wheeling through to the Ohio territory.[15]

Now, only the War of 1812 would temporarily stem the march westward.

CHART OF TROOPS GARRISONED

DATE	FORT HENRY	HOLLIDAY'S COVE FORT
July 17, 1775 [1]	(Still Ft. Fincastle) Lieutenant and 25 privates	N/A
March 24, 1777 [2]	N/A	"twenty five men" by order of the Council of War at Ft. Pitt; Isaac Cox in command.
1778 [3]	Gen. Orders Ft. Pitt: "Ensign Henry Dawson with 2 sergeants, 2 corporals and 32 privates to march by land to Holliday's Cove and Fort Henry to relieve the militia at those two posts…as whiskey grows scarce, it must be reserved for fatigue(d) men."	
Jan. 11, 1779 [4]	"small parties of the 13th Regiment at Holliday's Cove and Ft.Henry"	
April 5, 1779 [5]	"small garrison"	"small garrison"
April 15, 1779 [6]	"twenty five men"	"twenty five men"
April 17, 1779 [7]	"28 rank and file" under command of Lt. Gab. Peterson	"28 rank and file" under command of Lt. John Hardin
Oct. 13, 1780 [8]	"twenty five militia including subaltern and two sergeants" under command of Col. David Shepherd	"subaltern, two sergeants and fifteen rank and file"
Summer, 1781 [9]	N/A	"company of fifty men" commanded by Capt. Samuel Brady

Dec. 1781 [10]	"Lt. and one sergeant and fifteen privates of Washington County militia" (Lt. John Hay relieved of command on Feb. 1, 1782)	N/A
July 22, 1782 [11]	"only five Ohio County militia" under Col. Ebenezer Zane	N/A

Note: An inventory compiled by Major Jasper Ewing of Ft. Pitt on **July 25, 1778**, Indicates that Ft. Henry had seven boats on hand and Holliday's Cove Fort had two canoes.[12]

SOURCES:
1. Act of Virginia Assembly; see J.H. Newton, *History of the Pan-Handle* (Wheeling: 1879) 95.
2. Newton, 99; L.P. Kellogg, *Frontier Advance on the Upper Ohio, 1778-1779* (Madison: 1916) 303, fn. 2.
3. L.P. Kellogg, *Frontier Advance on the Upper Ohio, 1778-1779* (Madison: 1916) 453.
4. L.P. Kellogg, *Frontier Advance on the Upper Ohio, 1778-1779* (Madison: 1916)198.
5. L.P. Kellogg, *Frontier Advance on the Upper Ohio, 1778-1779* (Madison: 1916) 28.
6. L.P. Kellogg, *Frontier Advance on the Upper Ohio, 1778-1779* (Madison: 1916) 286.
7. L.P. Kellogg, *Frontier Advance on the Upper Ohio, 1778-1779* (Madison: 1916) 411.
8. J.H. Newton, *History of the Pan-Handle* (Wheeling: 1879) 109.
9. J.C. Lodbell, *Further Materials on Lewis Wetzel* (Heritage Books: 1994) 21.
10. J.H. Newton, *History of the Pan-Handle* (Wheeling: 1879) 111.
11. J.H. Newton, *History of the Pan-Handle* (Wheeling: 1879) 125.
12. L.P. Kellogg, *Frontier Advance on the Upper Ohio, 1778-1779* (Madison: 1916) 122 and 164.

CHAPTER IV

THE "PUBLIC" FORTS

For the purpose of this book, a "public fort" is one where Continental or "regular" troops were known to have been stationed in numbers. Such forts would have been "fitted out" at public expense, sometimes evolving from their more humble origins as fortified blockhouses. Generally speaking, the word "fort" preceded the name of a public fort (Fort Pitt) with the reverse being true for private forts. Holliday's Cove Fort is denominated as such herein, despite its clear public stature, to avoid confusing it with another fort in Pennsylvania, Fort Holliday in Hollidaysburg.

HOLLIDAY'S COVE FORT

The first shots of the American Revolutionary War were fired in 1775 in Massachusetts. Meanwhile, a different battle was being waged on the other side of the young country by the settlers of the Upper Ohio Valley. Native Indians, often armed by the British, were fighting to beat back white intruders from their traditional hunting grounds along the beautiful Ohio River.

Traveling by boats down the mighty Ohio from Fort Pitt in Pennsylvania, these pioneers settled along the first flat expanses they discovered in the coves and small valleys of the Northern Panhandle of Virginia.

This is the story of Holliday's Cove Fort, whose founding and tales of bravery have been left untold for too long.

If West Virginia was a state born of the civil war, surely its conception date was during our country's revolutionary period. Due to its strategic location on the Ohio River downstream from Ft. Pitt in Pennsylvania, numerous forts and blockhouses were built in the state's northern panhandle. Among these were Holliday's Cove Fort located in present-day Weirton, Hancock County,* and Ft. Henry in Wheeling, Ohio County.

Holliday's Cove Fort was named for John Holliday, an early settler and innkeeper on the Ohio River along Harmon's Creek. [1] In 1771, the settlement of Holliday's Cove was founded, about a year after Ebenezer Zane settled on Wheeling Creek.

Ft. Henry in Wheeling was built in early June of 1774 under the direction of Major William Crawford and others, and for the first two years of its existence was known as Fort Fincastle until renamed after Patrick Henry. Holliday's Cove Fort was erected in the fall of 1776 by a company under the supervision of Captain Issac Cox.** One text notes that Captain Cox had moved his family to Holliday's Cove in 1773 and by 1776 was commanding the fort there. [2]

Several other fortified, private "family forts" and blockhouses were built in the area around this time. In 2003 the West Virginia Division of Culture and History published *Frontier Forts in West Virginia* by McBride, McBride, and Adamson. That publication names Fort Holliday as the only known Revolutionary War era (pre-1784) fort in present-day Hancock County. Six other forts were listed as located in Brooke County: Fort Beech Bottom, Fort Bowling (Bolling), Fort Decker, Fort Edington (sic) Edgington, Fort Rice and Fort Wells.

As J.G. Jacob wrote in the *Brooke County Record* (1882):

> ... forts in some cases were recognized by the authorities and were fitted out at public expense, but much oftener,

---

*Ohio County was formed from Virginia's West Augusta district in 1776; Brooke County was formed from Ohio County in 1796. Hancock County was, in turn, formed from Brooke County in 1848, after a dispute concerning the relocation of the county seat in Wellsburg. The new county line was drawn through the middle of Holliday's Cove. West Virginia became a state in 1863.

**See affidavit of Francis Dunlevy discussed herein.

they appear to have been private property. The post at Fort Henry, and most probably at Holidays (sic) Cove, was of the former (public) class.

Harmon's Creek drains its watershed from both Hancock and Brooke counties and Forts Holliday and Edgington were located along this stream.

Respected local historian Mary S. Ferguson utilized family journals, diaries, and oral history to write the *History of Holliday's Cove*, privately published in 1976. Ferguson wrote that John Holliday had been commissioned by a council at Ft. Pitt to "select a site for a fort to be built at public expense." Men came from Ft. Pitt to build the new fort. John Holliday and Harmon Greathouse would situate the fort on Harmon's Creek, a tributary named after Greathouse.

> (They) had selected the place where the brook (overbrook) coming from between the hill crossed the trace.* The fort will be built facing the trace, the run would be handy for watering the horses and such, while the spring was only a step up the hill.

With the fort completed, John Holliday believed an inn was needed and built one just below the fort, facing the trail. The inn provided accommodations for the garrison as well as visiting military leaders. Shortly after this time, Thomas Edgington and his sons constructed Edgington's Fort "at a place called Williams Rock just above the mouth of Harmon's Creek," on the Ohio River.

While anecdotal evidence from newspaper accounts which do not cite precise sources is often suspect, several articles that appeared in the *Weirton Daily Times* and its predecessor, the *Leader-News*, over the years bear mention herein.**

In an article published July 22, 1926, in the Steubenville *Herald* entitled "Unearthed Skeletons While Excavating at Holliday's Cove,"

---

*A trace is a path or track left by animals. The "trace" was likely present-day Cove Road, known in the 1800s as Holliday's Cove Turnpike.

**Special thanks to Dennis R. Jones of the Weirton Area Museum for supplying several of these articles.

the paper recounted that three human skeletons were exposed while excavation took place in the grading of "Pan Handle Court." The account goes on to note that "…older residents believed that some members, at least, of the Holliday family were buried here, basing their belief on the fact that these bodies were found a few yards to the rear of the spot where the old blockhouse stood, which was in (the) charge of John Holliday…" A gravestone allegedly with the initials "J.H." had been found near the spot two or three years prior to the excavation. "The location of these old graves is across the ravine from the J.W. Moulds residence," the newspaper reported.

A July 23, 1931, article in the Weirton paper indicates that Holliday constructed his "blockhouse on a hillside where the present home of William E. Stewart is located." The article indicated that on the discovered tombstone were found the letters "J.H. JUN 25, 1787." The tombstone was located 20 feet from the door of the Stewart home on a ridge overlooking Cove Road. Its authenticity is questionable, given comparisons between the old newspaper photo and the stone in its current state.

In a subsequent August 18, 1931, article, the paper recounted that

> The blockhouse or fort was an oblong log structure of two stories. The second story extended out over the wall for a distance of several feet. This gave the defenders a more advantageous position…
>
> The Cove blockhouse stood near the present site of Clarence Melvin's home on Cove Road. It seems that the stream flowing down through the Mould's Addition was

*The Croxton's Run terminology is troublesome. Abraham Croxton is mentioned as an early settler in the area of Holliday's Cove. However, there is also a "Croxton's Run" located across the Ohio River just south of present-day New Cumberland. R.G. Thwaites, *Early Western Travels, 1748-1846* (Cleveland, 1907) Vol. IV, 104, Fn.65. Thwaites writes of the journey of Fortescue Cumings through the Ohio River Valley in 1807 and of his meeting a William Croxton who lived at his tavern with his wife and eight children, some eight miles below Yellow Creek. There was a Croxton's Run at that point that turned a grist and saw mill. However the journal describes this Croxton's Run as four miles above Brown's Island. See also the April 8, 1792, letter from the Holliday's Cove Committee to Col. Absalom Baird of the Washington County militia which differentiates Holliday's Cove and Croxton's Run.

called Croxton's Run* in the early times. The fort was built soon after the first land was taken up, which was in 1775.

Contrary to Thomas Edgington's 1845 interview with Dr. Draper (cited later herein), the 1931 newspaper article further noted that, at some point, the blockhouse was set on fire by Indians who "began to shoot burning arrows on the roof." The article, written by Clarence E. Stetson, *Daily Times* feature writer, indicates that the fort was rebuilt about 1790, and this new one was never destroyed. Wrote Stetson:

After the danger from Indians had passed, the building was made into a residence, serving that purpose about a hundred years. It was torn down about 1890... It finally became the property of the grandparents of John Wright, a well-known local resident.

Mr. Stetson wrote that there were "three blockhouses in the area: one at Croxton's Run, one at the mouth of Harmon's Creek, and one near the present village of Congo." These would apparently have been, in order, Holliday's Cove Fort, Fort Edgington, and, at Congo, either Chapman's blockhouse, built in 1784, above New Cumberland, or Greathouse's Blockhouse in Newell.

In an October 21, 1955, article written by Charles L. Campbell for the Weirton paper it was noted that Holliday constructed his fort "... on the exact location of the Ellson Stewart* house now on the hillside behind Overbrook Drive."

The article stated:

Holliday was a bachelor and had two sisters, Ann and Susan, who never married. He was an inn-keeper and his inn was situated on the site of the present Clarence Melvin residence at 611 Cove Road. The inn was a two-story building with a porch along the front, Colonial style.

---

*Ellson Stewart acquired this property by deed dated June 6, 1882, of record in the Hancock County Clerk's Office in Deed Book "E", page 326.

Mr. Campbell further wrote that "Dorwin Wright, father of Samuel Wright, tore the old inn down and built the house that is now the Clarence Melvin home."

The address of the Melvin property today is still 611 Cove Road in Weirton. The Kuzma residence, a stately old colonial style home located a few hundred feet above and to the rear of this location is most likely the exact site of the fort. The home is visible from the west bound lane of the Route 22 bypass in Weirton.

Saving Fort Henry

In August 1777, General Edward Hand, stationed at Ft. Pitt, warned settlers at Ft. Henry of an imminent Indian attack. Several hundred Shawnee, Wyandot and Mingo Indians attacked Ft. Henry, which was defended by a garrison of only twenty men. At the time, Holliday's Cove Fort was considered "strong enough to serve as a magazine," where "a quantity of ammunition for the defense of those in the country above Wheeling" could be safely stored. [3]

After a day's assault on Ft. Henry, the commander of Holliday's Cove Fort, Colonel Andrew Van Swearingen (1741-1793) and 14 men arrived, traveling by longboat south down the Ohio River, 23 miles to Wheeling by water.

During this siege Major Samuel McCulloch with his 40 men arrived from Ft. Vanmetre, located south of Holliday's Cove Fort. Cut off by the attacking Indians, Major McCulloch made his famous "leap" by horseback over Wheeling Hill.[*]

Col. Van Swearingen had been stationed at Holliday's Cove Fort by the Virginia governor to make repairs to the fortifications there and to defend settlers in the area north of Ft. Henry. The news of the attack on Ft. Henry reached Shepherd's Fort, located about six miles from Wheeling, and a messenger was dispatched to Holliday's Cove Fort seeking the aid of Col. Van Swearingen and his volunteers. An 1891 account of the mission described it as follows:

---

[*]This attack should not be confused with the later assault on Ft. Henry in 1782, where Betty Zane made her famous run for powder. See Hintzen at pp. 43 and 82. Eckert claims both events happened during the 1777 siege, pp. 131-133; but see, note 619.

They embarked in a large and commodious canoe, and worked industriously so as to reach the besieged in time to be of service to them. The men composing the expedition had all volunteered for the occasion, and notwithstanding the fact that rumors prevailed that an attack on their own fort (Holliday's Cove), in which at the time, the settlers had gathered in anticipation of it, was contemplated, yet animated with a noble and disinterested resolve, they determined to succor their unfortunate brethren, whose danger was not only imminent, but was already impending.

Departing under the cover of night, on the dark waters of the river rested an almost impenetrable fog, which involved the undertaking in great uncertainty and danger.

But they toiled and labored, although their disadvantages were great, often striking against the banks, running on the head of islands or coming in contact with projecting snags and the overhanging branches of trees, until at length they were compelled to desist from paddling and allow it to float with the current.

And this was a wise conclusion, for under the heavy cover of the mist, they might unknowingly pass by Wheeling and then be compelled to stem the current to reach their destination. As they floated lazily with the current, they beheld the light which proceeded from the burning of the cabin at Wheeling. [5]

Virgil A. Lewis, in his *History and Government of West Virginia,* (1912) believed "the defense of Ft. Henry was one of the most heroic achievements recorded in border warfare."

In an affidavit dated July 25, 1833, a Revolutionary War soldier, John Schoolcraft, who was seeking a soldier's pension, stated he had volunteered in February of 1777 as an "Indian spy." Schoolcraft indicated he served the areas between Ft. Pitt and Ft. Henry and worked from "Holliday's Fort." [6]

A beautiful 1940 mural painted by Charles S. Chapman (1879-1962) on the wall of the old Holliday's Cove Post Office (located on West Street in Weirton) is titled "Captain Bilderback's and John Schoolcraft's Expedition from Holliday's Cove to Fort Wheeling, 1777." Although it depicts a journey over land to Ft. Wheeling and not by longboat, the painting captures the essence of the rescue attempt despite omitting Col. VanSwearingen, the mission's leader.

John Schoolcraft is later listed as a "spy" on the roster of Ft. Lauren's soldiers, a fort on the Tuscarawas River in Ohio.

Captain Charles Bilderback is portrayed in later frontier events as less than heroic. Award-winning author Alan W. Eckert describes Bilderback as "a greatly overweight man with the reputation of being the type of individual who shoots first and asks questions later." Bilderback later led the senseless slaughter of the Christian Moravian Indians in 1782 in Gnadenhutten, Ohio. This massacre fueled numerous subsequent acts of Indian retaliation along the Ohio. Joseph Doddridge wrote in *Notes on the Settlement and Indian Wars* (1824) that Bilderback was brutally murdered by Indians, and his wife taken captive in 1789, in retaliation for his role at Gnadenhutten.

In September of 1777, John Schoolcraft indicated he was among the "few men under the command of Col. [Van] Swearingen who volunteered (and) embarked in a large canoe and proceeded during the night down the Ohio River, in the aid of Ft. Henry."

Upon their arrival in Wheeling, Schoolcraft and his comrades proceeded "to the ground where (Captain) Mason and (Captain) Ogel's companies were slain, found the cruelly mangled, buried them and soon after, returned to Holliday's Fort and resumed his business of spying through the counties aforesaid until December 1, 1777."

In the spring of 1778, Schoolcraft again volunteered as an Indian spy stationed at Holliday's Cove Fort, "under the command of Captain (Charles) Bilderback" and "made several excursions on the northwest side of the Ohio (River)," which was then hostile Indian territory. [7]

That same time period saw the aforementioned John Struthers (1759-1834) in the area of Holliday's Cove Fort. *In The Revolution Remembered: Eyewitness Accounts of the War for Independence*, Struthers relates the attack of "two or three hundred Indians on Wheeling Fort in 1777" while he was serving as a volunteer "spy and wood ranger," drawing his provisions from Holliday's Cove Fort. Struthers tells of volunteers scouring the "country ... from Holliday's Cove to Fort Pitt" so thoroughly for Indians after the Ft. Henry attack that "not an individual was massacred by the savages in that region" for the remainder of the year. [8]

Upon taking command of Fort Pitt on April 15, 1777, Col. Daniel Brodhead wrote that he had 25 men posted at Wheeling and "the like number at Holliday's Cove, some employed as artificers [blacksmiths], some as boatmen, some as wagoneers, etc." [9]

On May 13, 1778, Col. Archibald Lochry wrote that following the return of Col. Brodhead from his expedition against the Seneca Indians, several forts were evacuated, but Ft. Henry and Holliday's Cove Fort were still two of the "principal points garrisoned." Lochry would later be captured and scalped in 1781 by the Shawnee. [10]

An inventory list compiled on July 25, 1778, by Major Jasper Ewing indicates there were "two canoes at Holliday's Cove" and "one boat at Almond's Run between Reardon's Bottom and Holliday's Cove." This inventory would have included only property that belonged to the Continental Army, and not necessarily that which was under the control of the Ohio County militia. [See footnote 12 of chart.]

On January 11,1779, General Lachlan McIntosh at Ft. Pitt wrote to the Board of War that "small parties of the 13th Regiment (were) at Rairdon's Bottom, Holliday's Cove and Ft. Henry in Wheeling, all upon the south side of the Ohio below Beaver."

There were apparently cattle and a leather tannery at Holliday's Cove Fort in 1781. James Bryson, who had been arrested at Ft. McIntosh (downstream on the Ohio River from Ft. Pitt at the mouth of the Beaver River) for neglect of duty and disobedience for his alleged failure to "equip horses" while acting as a quartermaster, was tried before a courts martial headed by Lt. Col. Stephen Bayard at Ft. Pitt on June 14, 1781. Bryson offered as his defense that he had made efforts to fulfill his duties and, in fact, had requested "hides to make lash ropes" from Holliday's Cove. He was acquitted of all charges.

The inventory report, Gen. McIntosh's letter and the record of the courts martial were published by L.P. Kellogg in *Frontier Advance on the Upper Ohio, 1778-1779* , from the Draper Collection of the Wisconsin Historical Society.

In *A Genealogical History of the Dunlevy Family*,* Francis Dunlevy (1761-1839) gave a personal affidavit in which he indicated: ... volunteered on the 1st day of October 1776, under Captain Isaac Cox; his lieutenant was David Steele. His company encamped in the woods at Holliday's Cove on the Ohio River, opposite a large island, in what is now Brooke County, West Virginia, now known as Brown's Island, above Steubenville, Ohio, but below the mouth of the Yellow Creek.

Here the company erected a chain of log cabins, block houses and scouted, in pairs, up and down the river, for a distance of twelve miles. This fort or station was on the line of defense from Fort Pitt to Grave Creek; erected as a protection to the border against the Indians. [Dunlevy afterward remembered that he]... frequently saw at this post Colonel John Gibson**, of the 13th Virginia Regiment, who supervised the several stations upon the river.

This was clearly "the company of men from Fort Pitt" that constructed Holliday's Cove Fort that Ms. Ferguson refers to in her book. Eckert later puts Francis Dunlavy (Dunlevy) with Col. William Crawford on his ill-fated mission to Sandusky in 1782.

Unfortunately, no drawings of Holliday's Cove Fort have yet been discovered. In the case of Ft. Steuben, located across the Ohio River, drawings have been found. Nonetheless, it is easy to imagine how the fort looked based upon known construction of similar fortifications during that period. We know that a strongly built blockhouse or two would have been necessary to give Holliday's Cove the strength to serve as a "magazine" capable of safely storing munitions.

---

*G.D. Kelley (Columbus: 1901) 270.

**Narcissca Doddridge, in the appendix to her father's pioneer text, *Notes on the Settlement and Indian Wars* (1824) recognizes, as do most authorities, that Gibson was the "sole listener" and translator of the great speech of Logan, his alleged "brother-in-law." See Chapter II, *The Murders at Baker's Tavern*, herein.

The April 15, 1777, letter from Col. Brodhead further allows us to safely assume that the fort contained buildings for the blacksmiths, and boat and wagon builders he discussed. A quartermaster typically occupied yet a separate building, dispensing uniforms and supplies.

Nearly every comparison between Holliday's Cove Fort and Ft. Henry indicates both were garrisoned with the same number of soldiers from 1777 through 1779 (see table).

Eckert described Ft. Henry as "not a terribly large fort - - its spear-sharpened eight-foot-high pickets enclosed less than an acre of ground."

Regarding Ft. Henry and Holliday's Cove Fort, Jacob wrote that:

> ... they are described as consisting of one or more log houses, substantially built, with port holes for use in firing, of capacity to shelter several families and of the strength to resist backwoods assaults. These buildings, possibly half a dozen or so together, were surrounded with a stockade of logs set endwise in to the ground...

McBride notes that "Descriptions of forts in West Virginia (are) very rare." However, the authors noted that one is provided in DeHass' *History of the Early Settlement and Indian Wars of Western Virginia* (1851):

> Fort Henry was a parallelogram, having its greatest length along the river. The pickets were of white oak, and about seventeen feet in height; it was supported by bastions, and thus well adapted for resisting a savage, however powerful. It contained several cabins, arranged along the western wall. The commandant's house, store-house, etc., were in the center; the captain's house was two stories high, and the top so adapted as to be used for firing a small cannon. . . The store-house was but one story, and very strong, so as to answer for a lock-up (i.e., a jail).

It seems likely that Holliday's Cove Fort was similarly constructed during this same time period, facing the waters of Harmon's Creek with its greatest length. At Holliday's Cove Fort, sleeping quarters for soldiers (and settlers in time of insurgency) would have been needed. Officers typically slept separately from enlisted men and the blockhouses contained a second story from which to defend the fort.

The exact locations of Holliday's Cove Fort and Fort Edgington on Harmon's Creek, a tributary of the Ohio River, are easily determined from the available evidence. No doubt 200 years of flooding in the Harmon's Creek watershed has changed its course. In fact, a map of Holliday's Cove Turnpike dated 1838 shows a wide, meandering waterway. Photographs taken in the early 1900s indicate Harmon's Creek was much wider and deeper prior to the installation by the federal government of several flood control dams in the 1970s in the Colliers area. This project was then followed by the construction of the U.S. 22 bypass around downtown Weirton in the 1980s. The four-lane bypass construction rerouted the flow of the water along the adjacent hills and valleys.

A 1908 photograph of Harmon's Creek shows water roaring over a dam to provide power to saw and grist mills in the area. That area of the creek now has significantly less water flow due to the flood control dams built in its headwaters.

An aerial view today of Harmon's Creek shows its mouth on the Ohio River a few hundred yards north of the Veteran's Memorial Bridge, 652 feet above sea level. An area on Cove Road in Weirton, just southeast of the municipal building, provides the first sharp bend in the creek's course. A bit further upstream on Harmon's Creek, three miles from the Ohio River, today stand the aptly named "Overbrook Towers," on Cove Road. A small, seasonal stream still runs down the steep hillside from its origins near present-day Weir High School, and is directed under Cove Road through a culvert into Harmon's Creek.

An 1838 Holliday's Cove Turnpike map shows Given's Tavern then operating where John Holliday's Inn had been located. An 1871 map by F.W. Beers & Co. of the "Panhandle" clearly shows "Edgington's Station" located along the lower portion of what is now Freedom Way in Weirton, just south of the Half Moon Industrial Park. This would have been the site of Edgington's Fort.

Both Ferguson's description, noting that the brook passed over the trace at this point, and a description by Josiah Hughes in *Pioneer West Virginia* (Charleston: 1932) that "In 1776 Holliday's Cove settlement was about three miles back from the Ohio…," appear consistent with this location of the fort and inn as described in Twentieth Century newspaper accounts and the Dunlevy affidavit.

In the February 10, 1967, issue of the *Weirton Daily Times*, Mrs. Mary Campbell Bowman, vice president of the First Congressional District West Virginia Historical Society, addressed a local women's group. The lecture Mrs. Bowman gave indicated:

The (Oliver) Brown* homestead, which is still standing on the corner of Overbrook and Cove Road added to the beauty of the homes along this historical road. This home is reported to be dismantled.

The Old Fort Holliday (and) Inn were located on the hillside in back of the Brown homestead. It was there travelers stopped along their journey to Pittsburgh or Wheeling. The walls of the building had slots where the travelers' guns were put for quick accessibility when the Indians attacked the fort.

Given the fact that "boatmen" were present, Harmon's Creek would have certainly been of navigable depth from the fort to its mouth. The longboat used by Col. VanSwearingen would have been too heavy to carry for any significant distance on a regular basis. For safety considerations, being three miles removed from the Indian-traveled Ohio River seems prudent.

---

*Oliver Brown (1789-1880) migrated with his father of the same name to Holliday's Cove in 1792. By 1812, he had built a wool factory and sawmill in the cove. Brown is buried alongside his wife, Ann Colwell Brown (1792-1834), in the western section of Three Springs Cemetery. According to *American Ancestry*, Vol. III (Joel Munsell's Sons, Albany, 1893), 152, the senior Oliver Brown (1752-1846) was commissioned by Congress on January 16, 1776, and commanded the party that seized the leaden statute of King George in New York and melted it into bullets for the Continental Army. Another Pittsburgh record of ancestry indicates that the elder Oliver Brown was present at the Boston Tea Party. The senior Oliver Brown is buried in Brooke Cemetery. Oliver Brown acquired this property by a Chancery Court deed dated April 30, 1827, of record in the Brooke County Clerk's office in Deed Book 8, page 175. <u>See</u>, Forquar v. Colwell, No. 1560 (1817)

As is noted in *Pioneer Period and Pioneer People of Ohio*, C.M.L. Wiseman (Columbus: 1901), "Holliday's Cove and Brown's Island, Virginia … were famous places in pioneer times." Indeed, several soldiers stand out during this period.

In *Frontier Retreat on the Upper Ohio, 1779-1781* published by the Wisconsin Historical Society in 1917, Holliday's Cove Fort is mentioned several times. It was noted that Ensign (later Lieutenant) Jacob Springer, who was commissioned in the Ninth Virginia, "was the commander of the garrison of Holliday's Cove" in December 1777. [11]

According to the *Preston and Virginia Papers of the Draper Collection of Manuscripts* (Madison: 1915), George Cox served as an ensign at Holliday's Cove Fort for six months in 1776; Abraham Rogers served for "one month in 1776 as a militia man at Holliday's Cove on the Ohio frontier," and Jacob Walker was also in the service of Captain Isaac Cox's company at Holliday's Cove in 1776. Rogers was later a private stationed at Ft. Henry when it was attacked in 1777. As well, William Baxter served as a sergeant at Holliday's Cove in 1776 while in, the Virginia militia.

In the *Military Journal of Major Ebenezer Denny (1761-1822)- - an Officer in the Revolutionary and Indian Wars* (2007), Denny indicates that on November 10, 1789, he was headed up the Ohio River and due to the "high waters" had to "lay (over) one mile above Holliday's Cove," which would have put him near the mouth of King's Creek on the Ohio. In 1786, Lt. Denny had been one of the officers who negotiated a treaty with Blue Jacket and the Shawnee at Ft. Finney near present-day Cincinnati.

In 1779, Holliday's Cove Fort was staffed with 28 men under the command of Lt. John Hardin. Ft. Henry in Wheeling had a similar size force under the command of Lt. Gabriel Peterson. [12] Eckert claims Hardin was later a deserter in the Battle of Sandusky in 1782 and was murdered by Indians in 1792 while on a mission for Gen. Anthony Wayne in Ohio.

On May 13, 1780, Col. Daniel Brodhead of the Eighth Pennsylvania Regiment, wrote to General George Washington that he was preparing for Indian attacks but that the detachments at Holliday's Fort and Fort Henry had only "a small garrison to defend (the) posts, (and he thus) warned and armed the inhabitants...and assigned them an alarm post."

On October 13, 1780, Brodhead ordered the evacuation of inhabitants of Holliday's Cove Fort due to lack of provisions and recalled the regular troops to Ft. Pitt. He then ordered Col. David Shepherd of the Ohio County militia to send a "... Subaltern* two Sergeants & Fifteen Rank and file to Holliday's... Let them be supplied as the Regulars were and they shall be paid by the publick." Their mission was to act "offensively against the Savages." [13] Shepherd had been the commanding officer of Ft. Henry when it was attacked in 1777.

In the late summer of 1781, Holliday's Cove Fort burned to the ground. Contrary to the later newspaper accounts of "burning arrows on the roof," Eckert writes:

> The fire had been accidental and no one was hurt, but an imperative link in the frontier defense structure had been broken.[14]

> [The "accidental" nature of the Holliday's Cove Fort fire was confirmed in an interview by Dr. Draper of George Edgington in 1845 and appears in Draper's microfilmed notes reviewed by this author.]

Thomas Edgington (1744-1816), who had moved to Holliday's Cove the previous summer with his family from Pennsylvania, began the arduous task of rebuilding the fort.

By April of 1782, the work of rebuilding Holliday's Cove Fort was nearly completed. But it came too late for Edgington. He was captured by the renegade Simon Girty and a small party of Wyandot Indians near Harmon's Creek.

After his capture Edgington was held at Half King's Town (the principal Wyandot camp on the upper Sandusky River in Ohio) and

---

*A subaltern is a colonial military term for a junior officer and was used to describe commissioned officers below the rank of captain and generally comprised the various grades of lieutenant.

survived the running of the gauntlet. He was later sold to the British in Detroit and was eventually released a year later. After being reunited with his family, Edgington returned to Holliday's Cove. [15]

The *Sims Index to Land Grants in West Virginia* (1952) indicates a 935-acre grant in the Harmon's Creek area of Ohio County to Thomas Edgington in 1798.

Thomas Edgington is buried in Steubenville, Ohio, and his name appears on a Revolutionary War Veterans' plaque in the Jefferson County Courthouse in Steubenville.

Captain Samuel Brady (1756-1795), leader of the renowned Brady's Rangers, was 25 years old when he was posted at Holliday's Cove Fort in 1781. He fell in love with the daughter of his commander, Drusilla VanSwearingen. They were married in 1783. [16]

The newlyweds settled at Holliday's Cove Fort, where Captain Brady continued to command his Rangers. The Rangers were an elite group of volunteers, established in 1779, by order of Col. Brodhead. The eldest of the group was the aforementioned Thomas Edgington, age 35. The Rangers tanned their "thighs and legs with wild cherry and white oak bark... (and dressed) in leather legging, moccasins," and caps with feathers of a hawk to appear as Indian warriors. At times Brady's Rangers numbered as many 64 men. [17]

In a letter dated July 1, 1779, from Col. Daniel Brodhead to Col. Stephen Bayard, the commander of Ft. Pitt wrote:

> Captain Brady and John Montour have gone with a party to capture Simon Girty*, who is reputed to be lurking with seven Mingo Indians near Holliday's Cove. [18]

Dr. Draper's 1845 interview notes with George Edgington and John Brady reflect that Captain Sam Brady was in command of 50 militia at Holliday's Cove Fort in the summer of 1781.

---

*The mission was apparently unsuccessful, as the notorious Simon Girty would help Indians kidnap Thomas Edgington three years later. As an historical footnote, Captain Brady was said to have been "at all times a great snorer" while sleeping. His "nasal artillery" was said by one of his soldiers to be "enough to alarm all the Indians" in any given vicinity. See, J. A. Caldwell, *History of Belmont and Jefferson Counties, Ohio* (Wheeling: 1880)145.

Captain Brady is buried in West Liberty, Ohio County, West Virginia, about 20 miles south of Holliday's Cove Fort. His life is chronicled, in part, in the book, *Sketches of the Life and Indian Adventures of Captain Samuel Brady* (S. H. Zahn & Co.: 1891) which has recently been reprinted.

The End of an Era

The Treaty of Paris was signed in late 1783, and the Revolutionary War officially ended.

In 1786, the United States government constructed Ft. Steuben, directly across the Ohio River, only four miles from Holliday's Cove Fort. Its primary purpose was to protect government surveyors who were mapping the Seven Ranges in Ohio. Ft. Steuben was occupied for only seven months. Today the fort has been beautifully reconstructed and is a local tourist attraction. [19]

Once again, the former commander of Holliday's Cove Fort came to the aid of another fort. Andrew VanSwearingen "saved the whole survey (team at Ft. Steuben) by hiring out as a hunter for the parties for the ranges." [20] In addition to the venison and other game that VanSwearingen furnished, the commissary stores included flour, beef, whiskey, and salt, with bacon available at times. [21]

In 1792, despite the outward signs of peace, Indian attacks continued in Holliday's Cove. On February 4, 1792, the "Frontier Inhabitants Living in and Near Holliday's Cove," passed a resolution to be published in the *Pittsburgh Gazette*. The resolution told of an "alarmed" state of the populace and argued that the drafting of "frontier inhabitants to serve upon militia duty in any other part of the country but where they reside is … unjust."

A March 20, 1792, letter referred to Holliday's Cove Fort and Fort Edgington as blockhouses located at "… Croxton's Run and mouth of Harmon's Creek." It should be noted, however, that a subsequent April 8, 1792, letter from the Committee to Col. Absalom Baird of the Washington County militia stated:

Between Yellow Creek and Holliday's Cove a space of 15 miles will be uncovered. At present, indeed, we have twelve men at the station at Croxton's Run, being part of 20 men drafted from the militia of this county and destined for Holliday's Cove.

The language of that letter clearly refers to Croxton's Run and Holliday's Cove as two separate places. [See footnote herein at page 34, that the "Croxton's Run" terminology is "troublesome."]

The March 20, 1792, letter from the "Committee on Holliday's Cove" to Col. Baird warned that the "situation is growing every day more critical; the Indians have begun their depredations in our neighborhood (and intend) ... to make an invasion upon us." The Holliday's Cove committee asked for "60 men" to protect them.

An April 8, 1792, letter from David Bruce and William Ledlie of the Holliday's Cove Committee, noted that "A party of Indians have been discovered last Saturday night at the station at Holliday's Cove." No other details are provided.

In response, Col. Baird wrote to Gen. "Mad" Anthony Wayne that the inhabitants of the frontier had "gathered together in blockhouses, and are in great distress."[22]

In 1792, President George Washington appointed Gen. Wayne as commander of the U.S. Army of the Northwest Territory. In 1794, Wayne and his army defeated the Indian forces led by Blue Jacket at the battle of Fallen Timber. The victory prompted the signing of the Treaty of Greenville in Ohio in 1795. The Wyandot and other tribes agreed to move to the northwestern part of what is present-day Ohio, away from the Ohio River. [23]

Peace slowly came to the Upper Ohio Valley. On June 4, 1795, John Decker was riding to Holliday's Cove when he was attacked, tomahawked, and scalped by a party of Wyandot. He was the last white settler to be killed by Indians in Brooke County. [24]

By the turn of the century frontier outposts such as Holliday's Cove Fort were being dismantled or converted into private homes, having served their purpose as fortifications against the Native Americans who sought to protect what had once been theirs.

FORT HENRY

In October, 1776, "Ohio County was to all intents and purposes a military colony."[25] The heart and soul of the settlements along the Ohio River was a fort in Wheeling that would survive two well-documented attacks.

Zane Grey, in his classic 1903 novel, *Betty Zane*, described this famous Wheeling outpost as follows:

> Fort Henry stood on a bluff overlooking the river and commanded a fine view of the surrounding country. In shape it was a parallelogram, being about three hundred and fifty-six feet in length, and one hundred and fifty in width. Surrounded by a stockade fence twelve feet high, with a yard wide walk running around the inside, and with bastions at each corner large enough to contain six defenders, the fort presented an almost impregnable defense.
>
> The blockhouse was two stories in height, the second story projecting out several feet over the first. The thick white oak walls bristled with portholes. Besides the blockhouse, there were a number of cabins located within the stockade. Wells had been sunk inside the enclosure, so that if the spring happened to go dry, an abundance of good water could be had at all times. [26]

Probably the most historically accurate description of the fort can be found in the interviews of John Brady (son of Captain Sam Brady) and George Edgington (son of Thomas Edgington) taken by historian Dr. Lyman Draper in the fall of 1845. Dr. Draper's notes from those interviews include a hand drawn diagram that puts the dimensions of the fort at 300' x 250'.* J.H. Newton wrote that the fort was smaller and "covered a space of about three-quarters of an acre." [27] **

---

*Vol. 2S Draper Manuscripts at page 190 (Property of Wisconsin Historical Society.) Special thanks to the staff of Mary H. Weir Public Library who obtained on loan the actual microfilm for the author to review.

** An acre measures 200' x 200'.

Several undocumented pen and ink drawings purporting to represent Ft. Henry appear in history books. Wills DeHass' *History of the Early Settlements and Indian Wars* of *Western Virginia* (1851) contains one artist's notion of the Wheeling fort. The stockade around the fort appears to be of milled lumber, square on its face. The gun ports appear circular and almost decorative.

Construction in such a manner and with such detailing is highly unlikely for a fort built in the dangerous Ohio Valley wilderness in 1774, absent water-driven sawmills or the expenditure of extraordinary manual labor. Each log would have had to have been hewn by hand with an axe--all for no practical reason. Despite these apparent contradictions, DeHass maintains that the drawing is "a most perfect representation...of the stockade at Wheeling."

A similar drawing showing Fort Henry's stockade and bastions constructed of milled lumber (but with slightly different background characters) and with perfectly cut, almost decorative round gun ports, appears in J.H. Newton's *History of the Pan-Handle* (1879). The drawing's detail is also historically inaccurate, as the fort was likely built of rough cut, rounded logs which were pointed on the top. Inasmuch as Fort Henry was constructed in an especially dangerous year of Indian unrest (1774), the soldiers and settlers performing the task would likely not have had the luxury of crafting the stockade logs for appearance sake.

Establishing the Fort

The Wheeling fort was built in 1774 by soldiers sent from Fort Pitt. An estimate of the number of men present for that purpose ranges from 200 to 400 depending on the authority. [28] Originally known as Ft. Fincastle, it was renamed in 1776 after Patrick Henry, the patriot who was governor of Virginia. Historians put the location of the fort as between 10th and 11th Streets on the west side of Main Street in present-day Wheeling, West Virginia.

As the chart at pages 29-30 indicates, the number of troops garrisoned at the fort varied from year to year. By an Act of the Virginia Assembly on July 17, 1775, Ft. Fincastle was ordered to be staffed by a "lieutenant and twenty-five privates." The short enlistment terms of the militia and seasonal nature of Indian attacks in the warmer months of spring and summer caused troop levels to vary widely. Orders that troops be stationed at various forts were sometimes altered or never carried out. The "troops garrisoned" chart which appears at the beginning of this chapter gives the reader an idea of Ft. Henry's documented troop strength at any given time, although the Ohio County militia would have always been at the ready.

THE FIRST SIEGE

At the first siege of Ft. Henry, on September 1, 1777, it is generally accepted that Col. Shepherd commanded "a total of only 33 able men" within the fort, against an attacking Indian party of 200-300 warriors, mostly Wyandot and Mingo Indians. [29]

Reinforcements arrived within days: Col. Andrew Van Swearingen and 14 men from Holliday's Cove Fort, 20 miles north; Col. Joseph Hedges and Capt. Andrew Foits, with a force of 30 men came from Ramsey's Fort on Buffalo Creek; two companies of men under Captains Virgin and Boggs came from Catfish Camp (Washington, Pa.); Captain Samuel McCulloch and "upward of 30 militiamen" arrived from Fort VanMetre; and the ill-fated Captain William Foreman and his thirty men made the long journey from Hampshire County, east of Ft. Henry. [30]

The casualties in the 1777 siege included 15 dead and five wounded among the settlers. The brunt of the losses suffered by the militia had been caused by the successful ambush of two companies of soldiers under the command of Captains Ogle and Mason. Col. Shepherd estimated that 20 Indians had been killed, although no bodies had been found. [31]

Captain Foreman, from the Potomac area of Hampshire County, Virginia, was asked three weeks later to lead a party of 45 militiamen to check on the Joseph Tomlinson family, living 12 miles south of Ft. Henry, near the mouth of Grave Creek. To get there, the troops had to march through an area known as "The Narrows," a hillside trail along the Ohio River about 4.5 miles north of present-day Moundsville on WV Route 2 in Marshall County. [32]

On their return from the recognizance, the Foreman party was ambushed by Indians lying in wait; 22 of Foreman's men were killed in a matter of minutes and six were taken captive. [33]

Martin Wetzel, the younger brother of famous frontiersman Lewis Wetzel, then age 20, is said to have been along as a scout and to have warned Captain Foreman that the narrow path along the Ohio River bank was ripe for an ambush. Wetzel urged Foreman to avoid the Narrows and to take the "path over the hill," as he and a few soldiers subsequently did. Firing and yelling from above the attacking Indians, Martin Wetzel had sought to convince the Indians that a much larger force was present when the Indian attack began. Wetzel and a few others returned safely to Ft. Henry and reported the ambush. Captain Foreman and his men, originally buried in a mass grave, were later removed to a cemetery in Moundsville for final internment. [34] Martin Wetzel served in the burial party.

As the ensuing years dragged on, the Revolutionary War raged up and down the eastern seaboard. The fight for American independence would finally end in 1782 in Wheeling—in the last documented battle between British and American soldiers.

THE SECOND SIEGE

In a letter from Col. Daniel Brodhead dated October 13, 1780, to Col. David Shepherd at Ft. Henry, the commander of Ft. Pitt directed Shepherd to "order a captain and about twenty-five militia, including a subaltern and two sergeants" to Wheeling. [35]

By December of the following year, Lt. John Hay was commanding Ft. Henry, which was garrisoned by one sergeant and fifteen privates of the Washington County militia. [36] The massacre of the Christian Moravian Indians on the western side of the Ohio River at Gnadenhutten (Ohio) by members of Col. Williamson's party in March of 1782 left the settlers subject to retaliatory attacks. It would seem that the readiness level on the frontier would have been on high alert, but it was not.

Ignoring the impending danger, the Washington County militia was relieved at Ft. Henry in April of 1782. In a letter to Gen. William Irvine at Ft. Pitt, Fort Henry's new commanding officer, Col.

Ebenezer Zane, complained that "five militia are all the strength we have at present." With such limited defenses, Ft. Henry was vulnerable to attack. Indian scouts apparently took note. On September 11, 1782, the second siege of Ft. Henry began. [37]

In a letter from Lt. James Marshall of the Washington County militia to Gen. Irvine dated September 15, 1782, the size of the attacking force of the second siege is estimated to have been "238 Indians and forty rangers, the latter commanded by a British officer." [38]

Near Ft. Henry, some forty yards away, stood the fortified dwelling of Col. Ebenezer Zane containing military stores and ammunition that had been furnished by the government of Virginia. Betty Zane is said to have made her famous run for gunpowder to this cabin when supplies ran low during the attack. Ebenezer Zane's blockhouse was located near the present-day address of 1100 Main Street in Wheeling. It is clear that the Indian attackers were led by the British. Col. Zane wrote to Gen. Irvine at Ft. Pitt on September 17, 1782, that the attacking forces:

> … paraded the British colors and demanded the fort be surrendered, which was refused. About twelve o'clock at night they rushed hard on the pickets in order to storm, but were repulsed. They made two other attempts to storm, but to no purpose.

Informed by a messenger sent by the attackers that the enemy force "consisted of a British captain and forty regular soldiers and two hundred sixty Indians," the inhabitants of Fort Henry still bravely refused to surrender. On the morning of September 13, 1782, despite having driven away cattle and farm stock, the attackers disappeared. "Our loss is none," wrote Col. Zane. [39]

Fort Henry is said by some to have had an active frontier defense lifespan of nine years, fading from history after 1783. [40] Given the documented Indian attacks as late as 1795 in present-day Hancock and Brooke counties, it is likely Fort Henry's useful life extended at least a decade beyond the second siege.

In fact, when Holliday's Cove Fort, some 20 miles north, had been destroyed by fire in 1781, Eckert notes that "the majority of the residents from Holliday's Cove had come to Wheeling for protection." Short of Fort Pitt, there was simply no other fortification in the Ohio Valley capable of offering such sanctuary. That same year, Col. Brodhead and his "little army of about 300 soldiers" went down the Ohio from Ft. Pitt and assembled at Wheeling for his ill-fated campaign against the Indians at Coshocton.[41]

Eckert writes that in December of 1790, a settler named Daniel C. Whitaker survived an attacking party of Wyandot and Mingo Indians while hunting with companions – 14 of whom were killed – on Stillwater Creek, 20 miles into the Ohio country. Crossing the Ohio near Wheeling Island on a makeshift raft, Whitaker eventually "made his way up the bank and toward (the safety of) Ft. Henry," where several men ran out to greet him. This story by Eckert contradicts his claim that in 1784, six years earlier, "Fort Henry was dismantled on the grounds that the Indians had been pushed far to the west and the danger from raiding parties was now over." [42]

Instead, it is likely that Ft. Henry, or even a pared down version of the fort which had withstood two substantial sieges, existed in some form until the turn of the century, given the documented level of Indian activity in the Panhandle during the last the decade of the 1700s.

CHAPTER V

THE "FAMILY" FORTS AND BLOCKHOUSES

By 1776 the entire Northern Panhandle had fortified itself at the "neighborhood" level. A blockhouse built by one family became a safe haven for the entire community in times of Indian attacks, which largely came in the spring and summer of each year. As C.H. Ambler wrote in *West Virginia, the Mountain State* (1940):

Except for occasional encounters with Indians, "forting" was a life of monotony; days succeeded night in a continuous routine of watching and waiting.

It is necessary to have some understanding of how Virginia divided its lands into "counties" in the Upper Ohio Valley in order to fully appreciate its fortification defenses. On October 11, 1773, Lord Dunmore and his council at Ft. Pitt established the District of West Augusta in Virginia. The move was largely a response by Virginia to the establishment earlier that year of Westmoreland County by Pennsylvania, which also sought control of the Upper Ohio Valley.

The West Augusta area had been "a large unorganized, sort of Indian country." Ohio County was subsequently formed from West Augusta District in 1776. Brooke County was formed from Ohio County in 1796 and Hancock County was formed from Brooke County in 1848. West Virginia became a state on June 20, 1863.

As one French writer* described the Ohio Valley, the river was its "great artery" and the numerous creeks and streams its "veins."

---

*Hector St. John Crevecoeur, as quoted by Elizabeth A. Perkins, *Border Life* (University of North Carolina Press: 1998) 46.

These bodies of water were in fact the lifeblood of the early settlers. Most of these forts were located along major tributaries to the Ohio River: Raccoon Creek in Pennsylvania; Harmon's Creek, Cross Creek, Buffalo Creek, Short Creek, and Wheeling Creek, in western Virginia; and Yellow and Captina Creeks on the Ohio side.

Such sites assured the settlers of a steady flow of water and, in the case of most of the forts, access by boat to the Ohio. All of these streams are part of the Ohio River watershed. Not surprisingly, the map herein also shows a density of forts along the direct land route from Fort Pitt due west to Holliday's Cove Fort, as well.

In the appendix to *Forts on the Pennsylvania Frontier, 1753-1758*, (Harrisburg: 1960) a book which focuses on pre-Revolutionary fortifications, William A. Hunter noted just because "a 'private fort' is known only by tradition is no reflection on its authenticity, but… tradition can be a delicate matter." Hunter points out, for instance, that German-speaking settlers called "any log house a blockhouse."

There was, during the Revolutionary period, a clear distinction between local defense structures and "regular forts," with the former generally manned by volunteers. However, as noted on the chart comparing Holliday's Cove Fort with Fort Henry, local militia were often sent to relieve regular troops, thus blurring the distinction.

The following is a summary of known Revolutionary era "family forts" listed by present-day county boundaries that are familiar to the reader. They are generally listed as they appear on the map contained herein, from north to south.

HANCOCK COUNTY (WV) FORTS

GREATHOUSE'S BLOCKHOUSE

For the sake of completeness and to encourage further research, this blockhouse is included, although not generally listed by most authorities.

Daniel Greathouse, of Logan massacre infamy, is said to have built a blockhouse in the present unincorporated area of Newell, Hancock County, as early as 1770. In 1778, four years after the murders of his family members at nearby Baker's Tavern, Chief Logan reportedly shot and killed Samuel Muchmore "on the river in front of the Greathouse Fort" in retaliation. A few days later, Muchmore's widow and five children were said to have been kidnapped by Indians and taken to Lake Erie. One son, Samuel, Jr., escaped from his captors, while his mother and siblings were never heard from again. [1]

The Committee on Holliday's Cove, in its 1792 letter requesting more troops for protection, refers to the "blockhouse at Yellow Creek." According to George Edgington's interview with Dr. Draper in 1845, there was a chain of blockhouses on the *western* side of the Ohio in 1791 including one at Yellow Creek manned by Pennsylvania militia.

BAKER'S TAVERN

Baker's Tavern was the location of the massacre of Logan's family in 1774. Located across the Ohio River from the mouth of Yellow Creek, Eckert describes the tavern as "Joshua Baker's little cabin store," but states it had "obviously been strengthened." [2]

It was here that the perpetrators of the massacre obtained "two kegs of whiskey and a gallon jug of rum" to entice the warriors who were with Logan's pregnant sister, nephew and brother, and possibly his wife, to cross the Ohio River to the Virginia side. In his 1895 "new edition" of A.S. Withers' *Chronicles of Border Warfare*, Ruben Gold Thwaites describes Baker's as "a low grog-shop tavern" whose owner had been recently (in 1774) "warned not to sell more liquor to the Indians." The flat expanse where Mountaineer Race Track and Gaming Resort and local factories now stand was once called "Baker's Bottom."

THE SITE OF POE'S BATTLE WITH "BIG FOOT"

The mouth of Tomlinson Run on the Ohio is located near present-day Cowl Farm along West Virginia Route 2, only 2.5 miles downriver from the mouth of Yellow Creek. Today it is the frequent site of family camping and fishing trips on the "backwaters." Some 235 years ago it was the location of one of the most famous hand-to-hand confrontations on the frontier. The story of Andrew Poe's battle with an Indian known as Big Foot is retold in nearly every major historical book of the period.

Andrew and Adam Poe were brothers who migrated to the Panhandle from Maryland in 1774. In a *Listing of Inhabitants in 1781 in Washington County, Pennsylvania*, published from the colonial tax rolls by Shirley G.M. Iscrupe and the Southwest Pennsylvania Genealogical Service in 1991, Andrew and Adam were said to be residents of Smith Township. They were bachelors and lived off by themselves in a cabin; they were known as superb frontiersmen. Captain Andrew Poe commanded a small militia unit near Colliers, West Virginia.

George Edgington recalled Andrew Poe in an interview as follows:

(He) was dark featured—dark hair and eyes—(and) could easily carry a quarter cut of four green rails a hundred yards. He was six feet two inches, raw boned, and would weigh 225 pounds, and in his old age considerably exceeded 300 pounds. Adam Poe was of less size than his brother, but strong and heavy.

According to the great frontier chroniclers Joseph Doddridge and Wills DeHass, the Poes were part of a rescue party along with John Cherry and ten others in the fall of 1781.

The men were seeking the safe return of Philip Jackson who had been kidnapped by a band of seven Wyandot Indians after having just left Burgett's Fort near the headwaters of Harmon's Creek. Jackson was said in *Old Westmoreland* to have been a "carpenter, about 60 years old, and his trade made him valuable to the Indians as he could build houses for them." His son had seen the kidnapping and ran the nine miles to Ft. Cherry for help.

Wrote Edgar W. Hassler in *Old Westmoreland*, first published in 1900 :

Pursuit the same evening was prevented by a heavy rain, but the next morning seventeen stout young men, all mounted, gathered at Jackson's farm. Most of the borderers decided to follow the crooked and half obliterated trail, but John Jack, a professional scout, declared that he believed he knew where the Indians had hidden their raft and called for followers.

Six men joined him: John Cherry, Andrew Poe, Adam Poe, William Castleman, William Rankin and James Whitacre, and they rode on a gallop directly for the mouth of Tomlinson's Run. Jack's surmise was a shrewd one, based on a thorough knowledge of the Ohio River and the habits of the Indians.

Hassler based his account of the incident on a narrative given by the grandson of Adam Poe in the East Liverpool (Ohio) *Crisis* in 1891.

The rescue party, according to an 1845 interview by George Edgington, used "the very heavy white frost, the first heavy one to nip vegetation" to track the Indians. Poe's men caught up to the Indians just as they attempted to cross the Ohio River with their captive at the mouth of Tomlinson Run, just south of Baker's Tavern, near the site of Nessly's Blockhouse.

Doddridge wrote in 1824 that during the fight that ensued, "Andrew Poe had his famous encounter in the water with two Indians," killing one while Poe's brother, Adam, killed the other. Andrew fought in hand-to-hand combat with an Indian known as Dakadulah. After rolling into the Ohio--which was deep in that area along its banks-- Poe was able to drown Dakadulah.

This warrior with whom Andrew Poe fought was said by DeHass in 1851 to have been known as "Big Foot" due to his tremendous size. Eckert, relying in large part on the 1845 statement of George Edgington, disputes that, saying the Dakadulah and Big Foot (known for the huge footprints he left at the scene of raiding parties) were not the same man. The tracks that Edgington had seen of the Indian called Big Foot measured 13 inches long, and did not appear to be those of the same man that Andrew Poe fought.

However, the fact that a dozen militia serving under Captain Poe formed a rescue party and engaged in a ferocious battle with a Wyandot war party at the mouth of Tomlinson Run in 1781 is not disputed by any historian familiar with the subject (although George Edgington put the date as October 31, 1782).

All told, six of the seven Indians were killed, with the war party's leader, Scotash, the only one to escape. Scotash's brother, Scolch, was killed, and his body, along with that of Dakadulah, was recovered and buried by Scotash who returned after Poe's party had left to seek aid for their wounded. In addition to the death of John Cherry, two others in the rescue party were killed. Adam Poe was severely wounded, having been shot by one of his own party in the neck near the collarbone. The captive they had all sought to rescue, Philip Jackson, miraculously escaped unharmed.

Andrew Poe's right hand had been seriously injured when he raised his arm to block a tomahawk blow from Dakadulah, leaving him with a lifelong disability. He eventually moved to Hookstown, Beaver County, Pennsylvania—not far from Tomlinson Run—where he lived until his death in 1823. His brother, Adam, recovered from his gunshot wound and later resided in Massillon, Ohio until his death in 1840 at the age of 92. [3]

NESSLY'S BLOCKHOUSE (Old Route 66)

The site of Nessly's Blockhouse is geographically significant. It is located exactly halfway between the mouth of Yellow Creek and the mouth of Tomlinson Run on the Ohio—just about one mile from either tributary.

In 1785, Jacob Nessly moved his family from eastern Pennsylvania to the mouth of Tomlinson Run. Nessly established a blockhouse, grist mill and blacksmith shop there. Today, Nessly Chapel, founded as a nondenominational congregation in 1794, stands just north of the mouth of Tomlinson Run on West Virginia Route 2, which is also known as Old Route 66.

Jacob Nessly was a pioneer fruit grower and distiller. His farm stretched for acres along the Ohio River. He built Nessly Chapel from native stone, which he eventually deeded to its parishioners after moving to the state of Ohio. The indenture was purportedly signed on a boat on the Ohio River so a Virginia notary could attest his signature, since the body of water was the property of Virginia. The church later became the "first Methodist Protestant Church in the world," according to a local newspaper article.

Nessly was born in Pennsylvania in 1753 and served as a private in the Lancaster County militia during the Revolutionary War. He obtained land grants of 59 acres in 1787; 56 acres in 1791; and 128 acres on Tomlinson Run in 1792. Nessly is said to have grown several varieties of fruit on his farm, which he distilled into brandy which was then shipped by boat to New Orleans. The first communion cups at Nessly Chapel were made from melted silver coins he donated. [4]

In nearby Congo, William Hamiston is said to have operated a ferry on the Ohio River after settling in the area in 1795.

CHAPMAN'S BLOCKHOUSE (New Cumberland)

A state of West Virginia commemorative plaque on Ridge Avenue (WV Route 2) in New Cumberland notes the nearby location of Chapman's fortification, several miles south of Tomlinson Run. This small, fortified blockhouse was built by a wealthy new settler, George Chapman, "for the safety of his wife and children." Not much else appears in the literature about this blockhouse, besides Eckert's contention that it never came under attack, having served its purpose as a deterrent to the Indians.

Captain George Chapman (1747-1812) served in the 4th Virginia Regiment during the Revolutionary War. His wife, Johnnah, is said to have successfully armed herself and confronted a hired hand who attempted to rob the blockhouse while her husband was away on business. [5]

GRIFFITH'S BLOCKHOUSE (Weirton/Holliday's Cove)

The Griffith stone house was built in 1793 on the present site of Jimmy Carey Football Stadium in downtown Weirton, less than half a mile from Holliday's Cove Fort. The homestead was built against the hillside just below the present site of Williams Country Club on Marland Heights. It was said to have been used by early settlers as a fortification against Indian attacks and was torn down in 1932. A photograph of this fortification appears in Mary Ferguson's *History of Holliday's Cove*.

For the area, stone was an unusual feature, but obviously created a superior fortification to even thick log walls. The siting of the Griffith home would have given its occupants a tremendous view of the valley below, and thus any approaching Indians. The area below the blockhouse includes the present-day Weirton streets of West, Elm and Orchard. A roaring spring, a plus for any frontier homestead, running down the hillside still causes drainage concerns at the football stadium.

The dating of its construction as 1793 would have coincided with the February 2, 1792, and March 20, 1792, letters of the "Frontier Inhabitants Living in and Near Holliday's Cove," which were sent to Col. Absalom Baird, commander of the Washington County militia.

These letters, as reprinted in *The History of the Pan-Handle* in 1879, warned of Indians "who carry on war against women and children, and commit their murders at our doors and in our houses." The committee of local settlers, chaired by Richard Brown, complained that the militia "Rangers raised by the state of Virginia will not come up higher than Mingo Bottom," which was a few miles south, and the Holliday's Cove residents thus feared "from the dread of the Indians." This is further evidence of how the boundary dispute between Virginia and Pennsylvania during this period impacted the border settlers.

Col. Baird, in response to the Committee's letters, wrote to Gen. "Mad" Anthony Wayne on July 21, 1792 as follows:

> The Inhabitants of the frontier have either fled into settlements, or have gathered together into blockhouses, and are in great distress, having left their crops standing.

Although blockhouses were "already erected…at Yellow Creek, Croxton's Run and the mouth of Harmon's Creek," the Griffith stone house was clearly built as a result of the Indian unrest at that time. [6]

BROOKE COUNTY FORTS

SAPPINGTON'S FORT

Sappington's Run flows into Harmon's Creek near the current Brooke-Hancock county boundary line, high above WV Route 2 and the Ohio River. Eckert called Sappington's a "little fort" erected by the Sappington Family "a mile and a half up Harmon's Creek." Thomas Edgington was on his way to Sappington's when he was captured by Simon Girty and a band of Wyandot in 1782. [7] Eckert's description puts this fort between Edgington's Fort at the mouth of Harmon's Creek and Holliday's Cove Fort, three miles upstream on Harmon's Creek. Sappington's Run can still located on detailed topographical maps of the area.

EDGINGTON'S FORT

"Old Fort Edgington," as described in Newton's *History of the Pan-Handle*, stood on the Virginia side of the Ohio River, "opposite where Steubenville now stands." This fortification was located at the mouth of Harmon's Creek, near the present site of the City of Weirton's Water Treatment plant on Freedom Way. The Edgington homestead clearly appears on an 1835 map of Holliday's Cove owned by the Weirton Area Museum. An 1871 map of the Panhandle by F.W. Beers & Co., calls this area "Edgington's Station." The site of the fort (at "William's Rock") became a legislative starting point for the new boundary dividing Brooke and Hancock counties in 1858. [8]

As late as 1792, "The Committee on Holliday's Cove" was writing to the commander of the Washington County militia seeking soldiers to garrison the "Blockhouse erected at the mouth of Harmon's Creek," which was obviously Edgington's.

Edgington's Fort was built by Thomas Edgington (1744-1816). Edgington was a member of the renowned Brady's Rangers. He obtained a 935-acre land grant along Harmon's Creek in 1798. [9] Edgington is honored along with other Revolutionary War-era soldiers buried in that county on a plaque on the wall of the first floor of the Jefferson County Courthouse in Steubenville, Ohio, just across the river from the fort's location.

An interview in 1845 by Dr. Lyman Draper of Thomas Edgington's son, George, provided the basis for a great deal of material on the Edgington family summarized in Jared C. Lobdell's, *Further Materials on Lewis Wetzel and the Upper Ohio Frontier* (Heritage Books: 2005).

RICHARD "GRAYBEARD" WELLS' FORT

In *A History of Brooke County* (Wellsburg: 1975), Nancy L. Caldwell indicates that Richard "Graybeard" Wells "had a fort or stockade on his farm on Eldersville Road near the Pennsylvania state line."

The Commission to Locate the Frontier Forts of Pennsylvania, vol. II (Harrisburg: 1916) describes Alexander Wells' Fort on Cross Creek in Washington County, Pennsylvania, and then reports:

> There was another Wells' (Richard) Fort, about six miles northwest from (Alexander's), in West Virginia, a short distance from the Pennsylvania line. Col. Marshall, in a letter to Gen. Irvine on the 2nd day of July, 1782 informs him of the movements of Col. Williamson, then making ready for the expedition in movement against the Indians at that time. He says: "Tomorrow I intend marching whatever men may rendezvous in this quarter to Richard Wells' Fort, which is within five miles of Mingo Bottom; at which place I intend to stay, if circumstances will admit until I hear from you."

Based upon the foregoing 1782 letter, Richard Wells' Fort clearly was one of substance.

Richard "Graybeard" Wells also established a ferry across the Ohio in 1797 in partnership with his cousin, Bezaleel Wells, who founded the town of Steubenville, Ohio.

"Graybeard" was so named to "distinguish him from the other Richard Wells, who settled claims only a few miles away." His fort is said to have been a place where early church services were held.

Wells' Fort was also the place where the first school* opened in this region in 1777, under the instruction of Robert McCready. The same fort was a stopping over point for Colonel William Crawford's troops in 1782 on their way west to Mingo Bottom to attack the Indians at Sandusky.

In 1800, Richard "Graybeard" Wells is said to have fired his rifle across the Ohio River at a "lusty redskin on a large stone near the ferry, making offensive gestures to the ladies." Graybeard's shot killed

---

*Not everyone in the Ohio Valley was impressed with the value of formal schooling. Martin Wymore told one interviewer that "many of the boys were sent merely to keep them from wandering about where the Indians would catch them." See, Elizabeth A. Perkins, *Border Life* (University of North Carolina Press: 1998) 36.

the Indian "who turned an involuntary somersault into the river never to rise again." [10]

FORT DECKER

Located in present-day Follansbee, a West Virginia historical marker indicates its site along WV Route 2. Nancy Caldwell, in *A History of Brooke County* (Wellsburg: 1975), states John Decker's Fort was located "on Mingo Bottom land south of Broad Street and Main."

J.H. Newton in *History of the Pan-Handle* (Wheeling: 1879) wrote that John Decker was killed and scalped by Wyandot Indians while on his way to Holliday's Cove. Eckert puts the year of Decker's death as 1795, indicating "he was the last white man to be killed by an Indian in Brooke County."

Thomas Decker (relation to John unknown) started a settlement in 1758 in nearby Pennsylvania along the Monongahela River on Decker's Creek. During the spring of that year, a party of Delaware and Mingo Indians attacked Tom Deckers' settlement. Ft. Pitt's commander sent troops after the Indians.

A.S. Withers in his *Chronicles of Border Warfare* details how the pursuing party of 30 men from Fort Pitt "accidently came upon a party of six or seven Mingoes, on the head of Cross Creek in Ohio (near Steubenville)" which had been "prowling about the river below Fort Pitt, seeking an opportunity of committing depredations." The soldiers were led by Captain John Gibson, who was shot through the shirt, wounding another soldier behind him. A Mingo chief named Little Eagle was killed when Gibson "sprang forward, and swinging his sword with herculean force, severed the head of the (chief)." Two other Indians were also killed.

McGUIRE'S FORT

This fort is mentioned by Thwaites and Kellogg in *Frontier Defense on the Upper Ohio, 1777-1778* (1912). They wrote: "The site of the fort is not precisely known, but it was probably on or near Buffalo Creek, some miles above its mouth" on the Ohio. J.G. Jacob wrote in the *Brooke County Record* (Wellsburg: 1882) that "McGuire's was on what is now the Devinney Farm, north of Cross Creek."

Jacob should probably be considered more accurate in his description of the fort's location, since he was native to the area.

On August 13, 1777, Thomas McGuire, an Irish immigrant, and Edward Perrin, wrote to General Hand at Ft. Pitt from McGuire's Fort asking for help against the Indians, indicating they had at the stockade "about 20 men." [11] Thwaites writes that on October 15, 1779, Perrin was killed by Indians while hunting "on a stream fourteen miles above the mouth of Short Creek, since known as Perrin's Run." He was 50 years old at the time of his death and his granddaughter was interviewed by the famous historian, Dr. Lyman Draper, about his exploits. J.G. Jacobs wrote that McGuire's Fort could still be located in 1882 from "relics left" at the site by the fort's inhabitants.

COX'S FORT

Cox's Fort (or station) was located on the Ohio, and according to J.G. Jacob in the *Brooke County Record,* was built on "the bottom at Charlestown (now Wellsburg) just north of the town site." Garrisoned in 1777, this family fort was the residence of Capt. Ruben Cox, who moved from Maryland with his sons, Isaac, George, Gabriel, and Joseph. In a letter dated July 2, 1781, Gen. George Rogers Clark directed Col. David Shepherd to lodge a "considerable quantity of flour from two mills" at Cox's Fort on the Ohio River. [12]

Jacob wrote in 1882 that

> Cox's stood on the river bank about a mile above the mouth of Buffalo (Creek), but the site was a long time ago wasted away by the river and the town boys who for many a year picked up buttons, trinkets, tools and small pieces of money on the beach. All traces of the establishment were gone half a century ago. The road, however, then ran along the riverbank.

Isaac Cox, Ruben's son, would also command nearby Holliday's Cove Fort in 1776. As indicated earlier, the Council at Ft. Pitt garrisoned 25 men at "Cox's Fort on the Ohio" in the spring of 1777. Thus, it too was more than a typical "family fort." Gabriel Cox, another son of Ruben, would establish his own "Cox's Fort" in Union Township, Washington County, Pennsylvania.

In the fall of 1786, Cox's Fort was garrisoned by militiamen and farmers, such as Col. Andrew VanSwearingen, who supplied meat and produce to the soldiers erecting Ft. Steuben on the western side of the Ohio. [13]

In *Frontier Retreat in the Upper Ohio, 1779-1781*, Louise Phelps Kellogg wrote:

> Cox's Fort or Station was on the Ohio just above Wellsburg. It was the residence of Captain Ruben Cox who immigrated from Maryland in 1772. His sons, Isaac, George, Gabriel, and Joseph were prominent in early history. This station was garrisoned in 1777. [14]

FORT BEECH BOTTOM

Ft. Beech Bottom, located just below Wellsburg on the Ohio River, was manned at the direction of Gen. Hand at Ft. Pitt and thus, was something far beyond a simple "family fort." It was, as J.G. Jacob wrote in 1882, "… a block-house of some importance… as early as 1772," although this probably puts the date of construction a few years too soon.

Thwaites and Kellogg reported in *Revolution on the Upper Ohio, 1775-1777*, that Colonel David Shepherd wrote to Virginia Gov. Patrick Henry telling Henry he had ordered 25 militiamen to "Beach Bottom" in March of 1777. Thwaites and Kellogg indicated that the fort "protected the settlement of the Heuges family," but went on to erroneously state that it was "occupied only in 1772." [15]

Those same authors in *Frontier Defense on the Upper* Ohio, *1772- 1778*, state that Captain Joseph Ogle of Fort Beech Bottom wrote to Gen. Edward Hand at Ft. Pitt on August 2, 1777, indicating that Ogle and five men went in pursuit of a raiding party and "had a skirmish in which they killed and scalped one Indian." The Indians had "slightly wounded two Negroes within three hundred yards of Wheeling Fort." [16]

In September 1777, Captain Joseph Ogle was at Fort Beech Bottom with a company of 38 men and came to the aid of Ft. Henry when it endured its first major siege. On September 15 of that year, Col. Shepherd wrote to Gen. Hand at Ft. Pitt that Ogle was still "to support the Beech Bottom station..." Frances Duke, a "brave and generous man" stationed at Beech Bottom as an assistant commissary, had ridden to the aid of Ft. Henry and was slain. [17]

In October 1777, Gen. Hand stationed Captain Robert Shearer and 17 men at Ft. Beech Bottom. [18] On March 22, 1789, the Glass family took refuge at Fort Beech Bottom after surviving an Indian assault. [19] Undocumented genealogy sources indicate that the fort was 25 feet square, and it apparently was totally destroyed by fire in 1917.

Jacob wrote in the *Brooke County Record* in 1882 that Fort Beech Bottom was built near an Indian mound. Such pre-historic Indian burial sites are known to exist in the Northern Panhandle, particularly in Moundsville, Marshall County.

A West Virginia state historical marker along WV Route 2 states simply:

> Near here stood Beech Bottom Fort, which was with Fort Pitt and Fort Henry in the group of posts guarding the western borders during the Revolution and its attendant Indian wars. Troops from Fort Pitt helped garrison this important fort.

RAMSEY'S BLOCKHOUSE

J.G. Jacob in the *Brooke County Record* (Wellsburg: 1882) wrote:

> ... there was a block-house on Colonel Alexander Campbell's land, near where the pike crosses (Buffalo) creek, known as Ramsey's.

Eckert indicates that " ... a force of 30 men under Col. Joseph Hedges and Capt. Andrew Foits [came] from Ramsey's Fort on Buffalo Creek, six miles up from its mouth," to aid Ft. Henry in its first siege in 1777. Captain Samuel Mason, wounded in the siege, lived at that time on Buffalo Creek near Ramsey's Fort. Mason's sundry story is told in Chapter I herein.

Zacariah Spriggs and a slave known only as George, are said to have escaped Simon Girty leading a large body of Indians on a raiding party about five miles below the mouth of Buffalo Creek by seeking shelter at Ramsey's Fort in late 1780. Girty and his party crossed the Ohio at a point directly across the river from the present-day village of Windsor Heights in Brooke County. That point was thereafter known as "Girty's Point." These details and others that appear in *That Dark and Bloody River* about Ramsey's indicate that the fortification was an important place of refuge and very active during the course of the Revolutionary War.

RAIL'S FORT

Located on Buffalo Creek, John Caldwell (1753-1849) was stationed at Rail's Fort according to an account his son gave to Dr. Lyman Draper. [20] In Ross B. Johnson's *West Virginians in the Revolution* (Baltimore: 1977), John Caldwell (1753-1840) is said to have served "for a time" at Rail's Fort according to his Revolutionary War veteran's pension application.

SPARKS' FORT

William Sparks, a captain of the militia in General Hand's expedition in 1778, maintained a family fort which housed and protected settlers in the summer of 1781 when the family of William Boggs was attacked on Buffalo Creek. Sparks' Fort was located at the mouth of Short Creek. Sparks had been commissioned as an ensign at Ft. Henry in 1777.

Eckert, in *That Dark and Bloody River*, writes that:

A small fortified cabin had also been erected, just a few weeks before the Holliday's Cove [Fort] fire [in 1781], on the George Sparks claim at the mouth of Short Creek. It was being called Sparks' Fort, but it certainly didn't answer the needs that Holliday's Cove Fort had. [21]

There was also a Sparks' Fort in Westmoreland County (PA) which served as a place where voters cast their ballots in 1776 regarding whether or not to approve a Constitution. (See 1916 Commission Report, vol. II, at page 396.)

FORT BOLLINGS (not located)

A fort mentioned several times in the literature without its specific location ever being given, Fort Bollings (sometimes spelled "Bowlings") had been strengthened and repaired along with Holliday's Cove Fort by Col. Andrew VanSwearingen by order of the Governor of Virginia. [22] In *Frontier Forts in West Virginia*, McBride lists "Fort Bowling" as a Revolutionary era fort located "above Wheeling" in Brooke County, but gives no further location.

This fort is mentioned in the affidavit of frontier Indian fighter John Schoolcraft that appears in Lucullus V. McWhorter's 1915 book *Border Settlers of Northwestern Virginia*. Schoolcraft stated that in 1777 he served as an Indian spy stationed at Holliday's Cove Fort "watching the approach of the enemy and notifying the garrison at Bollings... of threatened dangers of the Indians..." Schoolcraft stated that volunteers from Fort Bollings came forward to join with those from Holliday's Cove Fort in early September of 1777 to rescue Ft. Henry, which was under siege. Unfortunately, Schoolcraft never describes the exact location of Fort Bollings. [23]

OHIO COUNTY FORTS

FORT VANMETRE

John Vanmetre established a fort at the mouth of Short Creek on the Ohio River, along the present-day Brooke/Ohio county border. According to Eckert, it was simply a fortified cabin located across from present-day Rayland, Ohio. It was located very near Sparks' Fort.

Fort Vanmetre is often confused by authors such as Peter Boyd in his *History of the Northern West Virginia Panhandle*, published in 1927, with the "Courthouse Fort" (Black's Cabin) located in present-day West Liberty, which is several miles east of the mouth of Short Creek.

In *The Revolution on the Upper Ohio, 1775-1777*, it is noted that Maj. Samuel McCulloch (of "McCulloch's Leap" fame) commanded "Van Metre's Fort on Short Creek during the Revolution, being shot and mortally wounded by Indians not far from that fort."

SHEPHERD'S FORT

Shepherd's Fort was yet another one of a number of "family forts" and blockhouses along the upper Ohio River. It was named for David Shepherd, who would soon command Ft. Henry.

On August 2, 1777, General Hand at Ft. Pitt wrote to David Shepherd, lieutenant of the Ohio County militia, warning him of the perilous Indian situation and ordering him to leave his own fort, six miles from Ft. Henry, and to rally at Wheeling all the militia between the Ohio and Monongalia rivers. [24]

In Ross B. Johnson's *West Virginians in the Revolution* (Baltimore: 1977), John Caldwell (1753-1840) is said to have served at Ft. Shepherd in 1777 according to his Revolutionary War veteran's pension application.

Shepherd's Fort was located on Wheeling Creek in present-day Elm Grove. The blockhouse and buildings were burned by Indians after the 1777 siege on Ft. Henry. A grist mill on the site was left intact. On January 2, 1781, Col. Daniel Brodhead ordered Major William Taylor to send "a subaltern officer (lieutenant), with a Sergeant, corporal and ten rank and file to Col. Shepherd's mill for protection of the same and adjacent settlements." [25] Shepherd's fort and mill thus became a "public" fort at this time.

Provisions were in short supply at Shepherd's. Only three weeks later, on January 22, 1781, Col. Brodhead wrote that the soldiers stationed there would have to furnish their own meat "until it may be in my power to send them a small supply." [26]

In *The Life and Times of Lewis Wetzel*, C.B. Altman indicates Col. David Shepherd had two sons and three daughters. His youngest son, Moses, born in 1763, is said to have married Lydia Boggs, the muse of Lewis Wetzel in his younger days. In 1798 the couple built a stone mansion on the site of the former fort which came to be known as "Monument Place."

COURTHOUSE FORT/ BLACK'S CABIN

Also said to have been "commanded" by Maj. Samuel McCulloch from 1777 to 1782, it was called the "Courthouse Fort" due to the fact that the Ohio County Court first held proceedings there in 1777 at Black's Cabin, "on the north side of Short Creek, about five miles from its confluence with the Ohio River," near present-day West Liberty.

Maj. McColloch, who was killed by Indians on July 30, 1782, near Fort Beech Bottom, is buried at the site of Fort VanMetre. [27] In 1851, DeHass wrote that the body of Maj. McColloch had been found with his heart disemboweled. An Indian later "told some whites that the heart of Major McColloch had been divided and eaten by the party. This was done, he said, that 'We all be bold, like Major McCulloch.' "

FORT LINK

In his *Semi-Centennial History of West Virginia* (Charleston: 1913) West Virginia University Professor James Morton Callahan wrote:

In 1780, near the site of Triadelphia the settlers erected Fort Link which was attacked in 1781.

This fort is listed as a Revolutionary War era fort in Ohio County by McBride *et al.* in *Frontier Forts in West Virginia* (2003).

FORT LIBERTY

This fort is also listed by McBride as a Revolutionary War era fort. Its exact location is not given.

MARSHALL COUNTY

GRAVE CREEK BLOCKHOUSE / "THE NARROWS"

Eckert writes that a fortified "little blockhouse" was erected at the mouth of Grave Creek in 1777. Located about 12 miles below Fort Henry, near present-day Moundsville, the fear that it had been attacked that summer caused Col. Shepherd in Wheeling to send two men on a spying mission. Days later, a company of riflemen under the command of Captain William Foreman attempted to reach the Grave Creek settlement. On their return after finding the blockhouse abandoned, Foreman's company was ambushed and massacred 4.5 miles upstream on a stretch of land along the Ohio River known as "The Narrows." In the ambush, 22 militiamen were killed and six were taken captive by the Indians.

Wills DeHass' *History of the Indian Wars of Western Virginia* (Wheeling: 1851) notes that just below Grave Creek was "Baker's Station" (not to be confused with Baker's Tavern or Baker's Bottom some 40 miles north). This station was established in 1775 and was fortified with a "stout stockade" at what is now known as Cresap's Bottom just below the city of Moundsville and the mouth of Captina Creek.

In 1791 a "large body of Indians" attacked a scouting party of settlers near the Grave Creek Blockhouse. A larger patrol of 18 men led by Ohio County militia Lt. Abraham Enochs was sent out. This company was also attacked and, although Lt. Enochs is said to have valiantly rallied his troops, his body was found the next day---he had been scalped.

Thwaites wrote that in October, 1776, John Caldwell (who was later alongside the infamous Captain Sam Mason when he was wounded in the first siege of Ft. Henry) was under the command of Captain William Harrod, and "was one of the party from Grave Creek Fort that went down the river to rescue the wounded and bury the dead of Robert Patterson's party, coming from Kentucky."[28]

In Ross B. Johnson's *West Virginians in the Revolution* (Baltimore: 1977), John Caldwell (1753-1840) is said to have served at Grave Creek Fort in October of 1776.

OTHER FORTS IN MARSHALL COUNTY

McBride listed the following additional Revolutionary era forts as being located in Marshall County without providing any other information: Fort Baker, Fort Beeler, Fort Clark, Fort Tomlinson and Fort Wetzel.

In the *History of Marshall County, West Virginia* (Marshall County Historical Society: 1984) Dale Lowe compiled a list of a dozen forts and blockhouses in that county. Although Lowe notes that some are listed "by tradition," i.e., oral history passed down from generation to generation, such local history is often reliable. Lowe's list also indicates dates he believes some of the forts were founded. According to Lowe, the Wetzel-Van Metre Blockhouse on Wheeling Creek, near Shepherd's Bridge, was founded in 1769—which would date the blockhouse earlier by at least a year than the date normally attributed to Ebenezer Zane's founding of Wheeling.

Here is that list, rearranged in a north-to-south sequence:

1. Wells' Fort (Middle Grave Creek) date not given.
2. Clark' s Fort (Sherrard) founded 1784.
3. Dague-Whetzel Blockhouse (Rt. 15) date not given.
4. Whorton-Enlow Blockhouse (Majorsville) date not given.
5. Wetzel-Vanmetre Fort (Wheeling Creek) founded 1769.
6. Beeler's Station (US Rt. 250) founded 1779.
7. Baker's Station (Cresap) founded 1784.
8. Martin's Fort (Mouth of Fish Creek) date not given.
9. Tomlinson's Fort/Grave Creek Blockhouse founded 1771.
10. Himes Blockhouse (Green Valley, Cameron) founded 1784.
11. Meighen Blockhouse (Rt. 74, Fish Creek) date not given.
12. Sockman's Fort (Rt. 74, Adaline) date not given.

SELECT FORTS IN WASHINGTON and BEAVER COUNTIES IN PENNSYLVANIA

The frontier forts of Washington and Beaver Counties are discussed in some detail by Dr. Joseph Doddridge in *Notes on the Settlement and Indian Wars* (Wellsburg: 1824; republished in Pittsburgh, 1912).

In 1915 and 1916, *The Commission to Locate the Frontier Forts of Pennsylvania* published two lengthy volumes. A map with some fort locations is contained in Volume II of the report. The second edition of the Commission's official report, edited by Thomas Montgomery, is the source of much of the following information. These "Pennsylvania" forts all played a central role in the revolutionary era history of the Ohio River Valley. They were for the most part located on the "land route" from Fort Pitt to Holliday's Cove Fort and were built along Raccoon, Cross and Buffalo Creeks.

BURGETT'S FORT

Established by German immigrant Sebastian Burgett in 1780 in present-day Burgettstown, Pennsylvania, a stone marker on Rt. 18 across from Our Lady of Lourdes Church marks the site of this family fortification. Burgett's name appears on Virginia land certificates as early as 1780. When the old log structure was finally dismantled, "tomahawk and bullet marks were visible." [29]

VANCE'S FORT

This fort was known for its early religious services. A much larger and more "famous" fort than Burgett's, located along present-day Langeloth Road in Burgettstown, Pennsylvania, it was established in 1774 by Joseph Vance. Vance allegedly helped plan the infamous massacre of Moravian Indians in 1782 in Gnadenhutten, Ohio. According to Dr. Doddridge, the massacre was instigated in large part by the capture and death of a local woman, Mrs. Mary Wallace, and her child.

In his pension application, John Struthers, whose story is told herein, mentions the murder of the Wallace family in the "settlement of Raccoon."

DeMay indicates that as many as 25 families "forted" at Vance's during times of Indian unrest. Vance's Fort is discussed in Montgomery's 1915 Commission Report. Joseph Vance is said to have come to Smith Township in Washington County in 1774 from Winchester, Virginia. He built the stockaded fort named for him. The fort was located one mile north of Cross Creek village on a branch of Raccoon Creek.

Vance's and Wells' Forts provided protection for a group of Scotch-Irish settlers who established a church in the area and met for worship as early as 1776. The Rev. James Powers preached a sermon on September 14, 1778, "under an oak tree just outside the gate of Vance's Fort." A brother-in-law of Rev. Thomas Marquis named William Parks was killed by Indians at Vance's Fort in 1782.

According to the Commission Report:

> In these forts (Vance's and Well's) social and afterward public worship was kept up for about seven years, especially in summer and autumn, the seasons when the Indians were worst to make their raids. [30]

RICE'S FORT

Most historians locate Rice's Fort on Buffalo Creek near present-day Bethany College. J.G. Jacob wrote that Rice's Fort "… was on the Dutch fork of Buffalo (Creek) in Pennsylvania, on the west bank of the stream." Its location was just over the present-day West Virginia-Pennsylvania border.

Published in 2003 by the West Virginia Division of Culture and History, McBride's *Frontier Forts in West Virginia* erroneously lists Rice's Fort as located in Brooke County, West Virginia, without providing any authority for such a claim.

Rice's Fort was well-documented by early Ohio Valley historians such as Dr. Doddridge. In his *History of Washington County*, Alfred Creigh writes that the fort "furnishes the most satisfactory history of those times" which he had been able to find.

In the Commission Report, it is noted that "about one hundred warriors" attacked Rice's after the failed siege of Ft. Henry in 1782. A September 17, 1782, letter from Ebenezer Zane to General William Irvine at Ft. Pitt, as well as a September 15, 1782, letter from Col. James Marshall of the Westmoreland County militia to Gen. Irvine both mention this assault on Rice's Fort.

The second siege on Ft. Henry in 1782 by Indian and British forces was better organized than prior attacks, yet still unsuccessful. Some 50 British soldiers joined forces with over 200 Indian warriors in this failed assault. Frustrated, some of the attacking Indians left to lay siege to Rice's Fort which was defended by only six men: George

Felebaum (who was killed); Jacob Miller, George Lefler, Jacob Lefler, Jr., Peter Fullenweider and Daniel Rice. Abraham Rice, returning from Lamb's Fort, was wounded badly.

DeMay describes Rice's Fort as "one of the most well known, and oft-used, defensive positions… of the western frontier." [31]

BEELER'S [BEELOR] FORT

This fort was established by Captain Sam Beeler in 1774. [Note: The 1916 *Report of the Commission to Locate the Site of the Frontier Forts of Pennsylvania*, vol. II, pages 414-415, spells the name of the fort "Beelor."] According to the report:

> What was known as Beelor's Fort was his own house, two stories high, made large and strong. The survey of 1782 shows no other…Beelor's house was the rendezvous for all the people of the vicinity in the time of danger.

The fortified home was located about five miles east of Burgettstown near Raccoon Presbyterian Church, some 18 miles up Raccoon Creek from the Ohio, in the present-day village of Candor. The journal of Rev. John McMillan indicates he preached in June of 1779 "at Beeler's place on Raccoon." Captain Samuel Brady and his Rangers are said to have killed a band of Wyandots who had attacked Beeler's Fort in 1779, rescuing three captives.

In 1781, fifty three militiamen arrived at Fort Beeler to be divided into smaller groups to patrol the frontier. [32] This would seem to indicate that the fort was of some substance.

Eckert indicates "Big" Sam Beeler designated himself as a "colonel" in the militia inasmuch as he was in charge of the fort. Volunteer militia posted at Beeler's included Alexander Wright and Timothy Shane.

In *Indian Wars Along the Upper Ohio* (2001), William Garbarino states that in the fall of 1780, "Robert and Hugh Shearer and two McCandless brothers were killed in Candor in Robinson Township, near Beeler's Fort."

In 1782, General Irvine at Ft. Pitt appointed Thomas Younkins as a "spy" working from Beeler's, although one author claims Younkins was at Beeler's Station near Cameron, West Virginia. [33]

It is worth noting that there was a "Beeler's Station" located in Marshall County, West Virginia, along WV Rt. 250, near Cameron. That fortification is listed in McBride's *Frontier Forts in West Virginia* and would have been a considerable distance (of over 30 miles) from its namesake on Raccoon Creek.

DILLON'S [DILLAR'S, DILLOW'S, DALLOW'S] FORT

Col. Daniel Brodhead at Ft. Pitt wrote on August 1, 1779, that "one Anderson who lived about two miles from Dillar's (Dillon's) Fort was slightly wounded and two of his little boys carried off by the savages on the same day mischief was done in Wheeling."

On July 30, 1779, Ensign John Beck, stationed at Holliday's Cove Fort, wrote to Col. Daniel Brodhead that a war party of Indians had attacked "Dillon's Fort."

As Louise Phelps Kellogg wrote in *Frontier Retreat on the Upper Ohio, 1779-1781* (1917):

William Anderson, a settler on the upper waters of Raccoon Creek, was surprised and wounded by Indians while at work in his fields…

An older son and stepson named Logan, four and seven years old, respectively, were captured and carried off. Anderson succeeded in reaching the house of a neighbor, who carried him almost two miles to the protection of the blockhouse of Matthew Dillon in Hanover Township, Washington County, Pennsylvania.

The older boy was returned from captivity (six years later) after the Treaty of Fort McIntosh in 1785. The younger boy grew up among the Indians, married a half-breed, and had sons, named Anderson, who became noted Indian warriors.

In his pension application, John Struthers indicates that "two boys at play (were) tomahawked and scalped… within two hundred yards of (Dillow's) Fort" in the spring of 1780.

In the 1916 map provided in the *Report of the Commission to Locate the Site of* the *Frontier Forts of Pennsylvania*, vol. II (Harrisburg: 1916), "Dillow's Fort" is located north of Beeler's on Raccoon Creek. A path connected the two forts. The Commission reported that Michael Dillow settled in Raccoon "before 1780." Matthew Dillow (unknown relation) was killed by Indians in 1782 and his son, John, was taken captive for several years.

Grace Fuller, according to the Commission's report, was a female slave who remembered "being in Dillow's Fort when about 17 years of age, at the time of an attack of the Indians, about the year 1778." [Report at pp. 415-416].

This fort was located in Hanover Township, Washington County, near Raccoon Creek on Clinton-Frankfort Road. It is mentioned by Captain Spencer Records in a narrative given in 1842 and published in Jared C. Lobdell's *Further Materials on Lewis Wetzel and the Upper Ohio Frontier* (Heritage Books: 2005). [34]

REARDON'S STATION

John Struthers, in an affidavit published in Chapter VII, indicates that Reardon's Station was somewhere north of Holliday's Cove Fort:

> The country traversed was from a few miles below Ft. Pitt, down the Ohio, crossing Raccoon Creek, Traver's and Tomlinson's Runs, Cross Creek, King's and Heoman's (Harmon's) creeks, near their junction with the Ohio, passing on our way down Reardon's and Holliday's stations where we occasionally drew provisions. [note: this is generally a north to south description of the company's journey with the exception that Cross Creek is south of Harmon's Creek.]

In a June 3, 1777, unsigned memorandum prepared for Gen. Edward Hand at Ft. Pitt, it is noted that an officer and 15 men were stationed "at place called Rordon's bottom about 40 miles below [Ft. Pitt]." This letter was published by R. G. Thwaites and L.P. Kellogg in *Frontier Defense on the Upper Ohio, 1777-1778* (Madison: 1912).

Those same authors printed an additional letter dated August 17, 1777, from Major Henry Taylor at "Rerdon's Bottom" to Gen. Hand which reads, in part:

> ...as the chief of the old posts was below Logs-Town [Economy, PA] I marched the men down to this post, and went down myself to the lower posts taking the minds of the people, and I found that everyone was for having it at the place they were....owing I believe to an alarm of some Indians being in the settlement, the inhabitants [are] in the utmost confusion yet it is as bad as death to think of moving.

Thwaites and Kellogg state at fn. 88 that "Reardon's Run is on the southeast side of Raccoon Creek, in Independence Township, Beaver County." Strangely, the otherwise thorough *Report of the Commission to Locate the Site of the Frontier Forts of Pennsylvania* (Vol. II) (Harrisburg: 1916) fails to mention Reardon's Station with the other forts listed on Raccoon Creek.

An inventory list compiled on July 25, 1778, by Major Jasper Ewing indicates there was "one canoe at Reardon's Bottom" and "one boat at Almond's Run between Reardon's Bottom and Holliday's Cove."

On January 11,1779, General Lachlan McIntosh at Ft. Pitt wrote to the Board of War that there were "small parties of the 13th Regiment at Rairdon's Bottom, Holliday's Cove and Ft. Henry in Wheeling, all upon the south side of the Ohio below Beaver."

The above inventory report and Gen. McIntosh's letter were published by L.P. Kellogg in *Frontier Advance on the Upper Ohio, 1778-1779* (Madison: 1916) at pages 122 and 198.

DODDRIDGE'S FORT

Jacob wrote that this was a Brooke County fort built "... on the hill overlooking the bottom at Charlestown (Wellsburg)." However, the *Commission to Locate the Frontier Forts of Pennsylvania* (Harrisburg: 1915) locates Doddridge's Fort in Washington County, Pennsylvania, on the north branch of Buffalo Creek, not in West Virginia.

Doddridge's Fort was named for John Doddridge, and is described in the Commission's Report as being erected on Buffalo Creek, "about three-fourths of a mile southwest from Teeter's Fort." The Commission's 1916 map locates it in the Keystone State just over the present-day West Virginia-Pennsylvania state line. According to the Report:

> When this fort was built, it probably took the place of Teeter's Fort, which had become indefensible... the stockade enclosed about one-half an acre of land (including) an excellent spring...

The fort is said to have protected "twelve surrounding families and the central blockhouse was still standing in 1913." [35]

COX'S STATION (PA)

There was also a second "Cox's Fort" in Union Township in Washington County, Pennsylvania. It was built when the Virginia-Pennsylvania border dispute still put these lands under the Virginia land office. This Fort Cox was established by Virginia militia Major Gabriel Cox (son of Wellsburg's Ruben Cox) and was active from at least 1778 to 1780. Dr. Joseph Doddridge wrote that it was located "near the Monongahela River, ... on Peter's Creek in Peter's Township, one mile from Gastonville and 14 miles (due south) from Pittsburgh."

According to the Commission Report, Cox's Station was in existence well before the end of the Revolutionary War. The fort was the location of a "rendezvous" between militia and regular army troops in March of 1778. [36]

ALEXANDER WELLS' FORT

The 1916 Commission Report indicates Alexander Wells' Fort was built in 1780 on the waters of Cross Creek in Washington County. It served as a "refuge for families (and) also as a defense for the flour mill" which operated nearby. Alexander Wells' Fort was located in Pennsylvania about six miles northwest of Richard "Graybeard" Wells' Fort in present-day West Virginia.

In the spring of 1782, the inhabitants of Alexander Wells' Fort, including John Sappington, George McCulloch and John and Benjamin Biggs, wrote a letter to Gen. William Irvine at Ft. Pitt asking for soldiers to be stationed there to protect the mill and the local families. [37] John Sappington was implicated in the murders at Baker's Tavern as discussed herein.

HOAGLAND'S FORT

According to the *Report of the Commission to Locate the Site of The Frontier Forts of Western Pennsylvania*, Volume II (Harrisburg: 1916), Hoagland's Fort was built by Henry Hoagland on the north branch of Raccoon Creek in Smith Township, Washington County. Matthew, Thomas and William Rankin, along with James Leech, are said to have "forted" there.

There is an old frontier tale that the women of Hoagland's Fort once repulsed an Indian attack by using scalding water. [38]

The fort is mentioned by Boyd Crumrine in the *History of Washington County* (Philadelphia: 1882). It is also alluded to in the pension narrative of John Struthers detailed herein:

> In the spring of 1778 ... the whole settlement, from Wheeling upwards, was broken up and retired into forts ...from the paucity of males in each they could spare none to act as spies or wood rangers...on my return from an ineffectual scout in my pursuit of the savages [who had committed several murders on Ten Mile Creek]...a request was sent to me from Hoagland's Fort to turn out with as many volunteers as I could collect... (and although among the youngest) I was elected to head about fifteen or sixteen active and brave men...

FORT CHERRY

Located near McDonald, Pennsylvania, close to a high school whose name memorializes Fort Cherry, this fort "consisted of three log buildings, one twenty-five feet square, the others smaller. They were arranged in a triangular form and enclosed with a stockade...the large building was two stories in height, with a half story above, and was built to withstand a formidable attack." The fort was situated on the Cherry farm, on little Raccoon Creek, and was constructed in the fall and summer of 1774. [39]

The fort had been founded by John Cherry, who "was a man of great popularity, and a natural leader on the frontier." Doddridge claims Cherry was slain in 1781 near the mouth of Tomlinson Run, during Poe's famous fight with "Big Foot" while rescuing a kidnapped settler. [40] Eckert believes the slain man was named "Thomas" Cherry, relying upon George Edgington's 1845 interview. See the story of Poe's battle herein.

LOGSTOWN

Logstown is best known for being a major Indian village of the Delaware and Shawnee. It also served as a trading post on the Ohio River below Ft. Pitt prior to the French and Indian War. Logstown was located near the present Beaver County village of Economy, just off I-79 as the interstate crosses the Ohio River. George Washington stayed at Logstown from November 24 to December 1 in 1753.

In 1752 a treaty conference was held at Logstown. The agreement reached there between the English and the Indians was short-lived. The Virginia party to the negotiations included Christopher Gist acting on behalf of the Ohio Company, with Andrew Montour acting as interpreter. Representatives of the Delaware tribe were met at Shannopin's Town and were then transported on four canoes down the Ohio to Logstown.

At a point opposite the Delaware's town where Queen Aliquippa lived, they were again received with much ceremony. On May 31 the party arrived at Logstown where they awaited the late arrival of the Half-King of the Senecas...Montour as the English mouthpiece spoke briefly to each the Delaware, Shawnee and Wyandot... the new treaty included the recognition by the Indians of Virginia's claims...and guaranteed the Ohio Company the privilege of establishing settlements...[41]

Within a year, however, at the instigation of the French who had been left out of the negotiations, the terms of the Treaty of Logstown were being disregarded.

Logstown is included in this list of Revolutionary era forts and blockhouses due to the fact that on March 24, 1777, a Council of War at Ft. Pitt determined that Col. William Crawford should "station twenty-five men (each) at Logstown, Holliday's Cove (Weirton, WV) and Cox's (Wellsburg, WV) upon the Ohio," indicating its role as a Revolutionary era fortification along that river.

REDSTONE OLD FORT

This Pre-Revolutionary fort was located along the Monongahela River at the site of present-day Brownsville, PA. It is included in this list because of its geographical location: due east of Wheeling by land. Thus, many settlers, including the venerable Ebenezer Zane, used Redstone Old Fort as a staging area in their migration west to the Ohio Valley.

The Commission Report describes Redstone as a "log house 39 feet square," and the drawing contained in the report shows bastions at each corner along with a wide "ditch" around the entire fort with a draw bridge. The fort was later known as Fort Burd and was first occupied in February, 1754, by Captain Trent for the Ohio Company. It was used as a strong storehouse for supplies and ammunition. It was considered a strategic location below Pittsburgh during the French and Indian War.

GREENE COUNTY (PA)

RYERSON'S STATION

Ryerson's Station (or Fort) is described in the Commission Report as being located in Greene County, Pennsylvania, "at the north branch of Dunkard Creek" which is one of the headwaters of Wheeling Creek. In 1790, the Davis family was attacked at their nearby home by a party of Indians. The father and two sons were killed as they ate breakfast. Another son was out gathering horses. The mother and daughter were taken captive. A neighboring settler, John Henderson, shot and killed one of the Indians whose skeleton was found years later. The "decaying body of the daughter was found, but no trace of the mother was ever discovered," according to the 1916 report.

James Paull was said was said to have "commanded a company of scouts or rangers" at Ryerson's in 1784. According to the Commission Report, "Ryerson's Fort [was] "an important rallying point in times of danger, as it was located on the great Indian war path leading from across the Ohio river to the Monongahela."

Eckert indicates that in late 1780, Col. Samuel Beeler, from a fort on Raccoon*; Joseph Tomlinson, from the Grave Creek Blockhouse; and William Ryerson, of Ryerson's Station on the headwaters of Wheeling Creek, made a long and difficult journey across Pennsylvania to educate leaders in Philadelphia of the serious and deadly Indian situation in the Ohio Valley. The officers there sympathized with the three men and promised to furnish aid. [42]

---

*Scott Powell in *History of Marshall County* (Moundsville: 1925) claims the 1780 trip was made by "Colonel Beeler" of Beeler's Station near Cameron, WV. Given the proximity of this fort to Grave Creek and Ryerson's Station, Powell's claim seems credible.

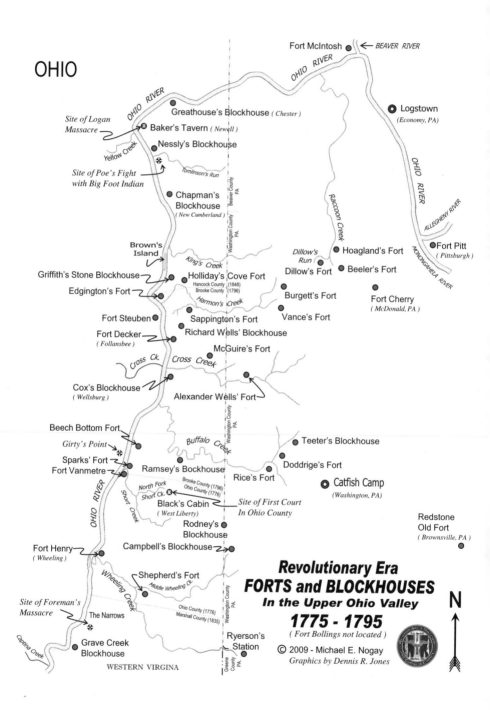

OHIO

Fort McIntosh ● ← *BEAVER RIVER*

OHIO RIVER

OHIO RIVER

Greathouse's Blockhouse (*Chester*)

Site of Logan Massacre

Baker's Tavern (*Newell*)

Nessly's Blockhouse

Yellow Creek

Tomlinson's Run

Site of Poe's Fight with Big Foot Indian

Chapman's Blockhouse (*New Cumberland*)

Logstown ● *(Economy, PA)*

OHIO RIVER

Raccoon Creek

ALLEGHENY RIVER

Beaver County PA
Washington County PA

Brown's Island

Griffith's Stone Blockhouse

Edgington's Fort

King's Creek

Holliday's Cove Fort
Hancock County (1848)
Brooke County (1796)

Harmon's Creek

Dillow's Run

Dillow's Fort ●

Hoagland's Fort ●

Beeler's Fort ●

● Fort Pitt (*Pittsburgh*)

MONONGAHELA RIVER

Burgett's Fort ●

Fort Cherry ● (*McDonald, PA*)

Fort Steuben ●

Sappington's Fort ●

Vance's Fort ●

Fort Decker (*Follansbee*)

Richard Wells' Blockhouse

McGuire's Fort

Cross Ck.   *Cross Creek*

Cox's Blockhouse (*Wellsburg*)

Alexander Wells' Fort

Beech Bottom Fort

Girty's Point

Sparks' Fort
Fort Vanmetre

Ramsey's Bockhouse

Buffalo Creek

Teeter's Blockhouse ●

Doddrige's Fort ●

Rice's Fort ●

Washington County PA

North Fork
Brooke County (1796)
Ohio County (1776)
Short Ck.

Black's Cabin (*West Liberty*)

Site of First Court In Ohio County

Catfish Camp ● *(Washington, PA)*

Rodney's Blockhouse

Fort Henry (*Wheeling*)

Campbell's Blockhouse

OHIO RIVER   *Short Creek*

Redstone Old Fort (*Brownsville, PA*) ●

Shepherd's Fort

Wheeling Creek   *Middle Wheeling Ck.*

Site of Foreman's Massacre   The Narrows

Ohio County (1776)
Marshall County (1835)

Washington County PA

Revolutionary Era
FORTS and BLOCKHOUSES
In the Upper Ohio Valley

1775 - 1795

Captina Creek

Grave Creek Blockhouse

WESTERN VIRGINA

Ryerson's Station

Greene County PA

(*Fort Bollings not located*)

© 2009 - Michael E. Nogay
Graphics by Dennis R. Jones

N ↑

- 86 -

CHAPTER VI

CONTINENTAL and MILITIA TROOPS
(1775-1788)

The relationship between the "regular" or continental troops and each colony's militia was much different in 1776 than exists today between the United States Army and the National Guard of each state.

The United States Constitution, with its "Supremacy Clause" declaring the laws of the federal government "supreme" to state laws, was not adopted until 1788. For the 12 years after the Continental Congress declared America's independence in 1776, the states were clearly in control of the militia, not the federal government. With state boundary lines further blurred by conflicts between Pennsylvania and Virginia in their efforts to control the area near Ft. Pitt and the Ohio Valley, militia protection along the frontier was at times haphazard.

The second Continental Congress adopted the Articles of Confederation in November of 1777, whereby each state retained its sovereign power. Under the Articles, state militia officers and troops were independent of federal control. In fact, the federal government did not even have the ability to levy taxes. Governors of states controlled the militia, not Congress. This, of course, in no way meant that state militia troops were well-equipped or paid. Such state soldiers were even expected to provide their own guns and blankets. The fact that 50 years later many of these brave militiamen who served on the Ohio frontier would be denied Revolutionary war pensions only added insult to injury.

A colonel of the Continental Army had no actual authority over a captain of the state militia troops in the years prior to 1788. The self-proclaimed commander of a "family" fort could—and often did--call himself a "colonel," even though he had little or no military training,

Congress chose a Virginia state soldier, George Washington, to command and general the Continental Army. States such as Virginia furnished troops to the Continental Army while also maintaining their own militia troops. In 1778, Secretary of War Henry Knox estimated that Virginia furnished 5,230 Continental troops while maintaining 2,000 militia troops. [1]

The militia (or "millishy" as they called themselves) were expert marksmen with an "attitude problem." The militia soldier might abandon his assigned post without a moment's notice if family concerns called him home. Often in the great "expeditions" into Indian territory, the only reward for militia soldiers was the plunder they looted from their victims or the bounties they were paid for Indian scalps.

Militia units were organized at the county level. According to the militia laws of Pennsylvania and Virginia "each company was commanded by a colonel, lieutenant colonel and major; and the whole by a county lieutenant." For the time period generally covered by this book, David Shepherd served as the lieutenant of the Ohio county militia in the Northern Panhandle.

When Brig. Gen. William Irvine assumed command of the troops at Ft. Pitt, he found the fort in need of serious repairs and the garrison in a "mutinous condition."

On December 2, 1781, Irvine wrote to Gen. George Washington that he had placed the Pennsylvania forces at Ft. Pitt under the command of Lt. Col. Stephen Bayard [not to be confused with Col. Absalom Baird of the Washington County, Pennsylvania militia]. The Virginia forces were under the control of Col. John Gibson, who had previously taken command of Ft. Pitt from Col. Daniel Brodhead that summer. Irvine found the fort and its troops in a "wretched state," and wrote:

I never saw troops cut so truly a deplorable, and at the same time despicable, figure. Indeed, when I arrived, no man would believe from their appearance that they were soldiers; nay, it would be difficult to determine they were white men.

By March of 1775, the Virginia legislature had provided for a state militia "but not [for] the garrisons of the frontier forts." In July of that year, the Continental Congress organized three departments of Indian affairs "of which the Pittsburgh and Western Virginia region constituted the central (department)." [2]

In 1778 the Continental Congress voted to raise a militia in Virginia and Pennsylvania "for the protection and operation of the Western frontiers." This was an important development for the beleaguered settlers.

Each non-commissioned officer and soldier was "to receive twenty dollars bounty and [the] same clothing [as] the other Continental soldiers" for their one year's tour of duty. However, each of these soldiers had to supply "his own blanket, musket or rifle and accoutrements." The same resolution gave Gen. George Washington authority to appoint the commander of Ft. Pitt and the "quartermaster, commissary and paymaster" of the various militias – thus exercising a degree of control over these state soldiers. [3]

The Revolutionary War would, after all, be defended on two vastly different fronts against two vastly different enemies.

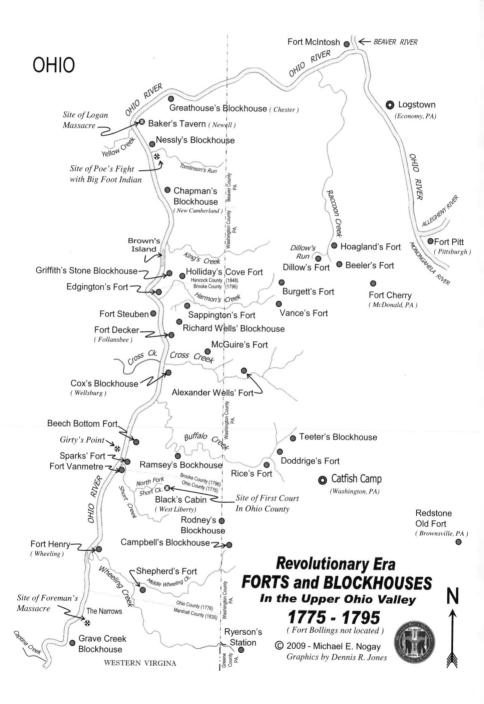

OHIO

Fort McIntosh ← BEAVER RIVER

OHIO RIVER

OHIO RIVER

Site of Logan
Massacre

Greathouse's Blockhouse (Chester)

Baker's Tavern (Newell)

Nessly's Blockhouse

Yellow Creek

Site of Poe's Fight
with Big Foot Indian

Tomlinson's Run

Chapman's
Blockhouse
(New Cumberland)

Beaver County
PA

Washington County
PA

Logstown
(Economy, PA)

OHIO RIVER

ALLEGHENY RIVER

Raccoon Creek

Brown's
Island

King's Creek

Griffith's Stone Blockhouse

Holliday's Cove Fort
Hancock County (1848)
Brooke County (1796)

Edgington's Fort

Harmon's Creek

Fort Steuben

Sappington's Fort

Fort Decker
(Follansbee)

Richard Wells' Blockhouse

McGuire's Fort

Cross Ck.

Cross Creek

Cox's Blockhouse
(Wellsburg)

Alexander Wells' Fort

Dillow's
Run

Hoagland's Fort

Dillow's Fort

Beeler's Fort

Burgett's Fort

Vance's Fort

Fort Pitt
(Pittsburgh)

MONONGAHELA RIVER

Fort Cherry
(McDonald, PA)

Beech Bottom Fort

Girty's Point

Sparks' Fort
Fort Vanmetre

Ramsey's Bockhouse

North Fork
Short Ck.

Black's Cabin
(West Liberty)

Rodney's
Blockhouse

Fort Henry
(Wheeling)

Campbell's Blockhouse

Buffalo Creek

Washington County
PA

Brooke County (1796)
Ohio County (1776)

Site of First Court
In Ohio County

Teeter's Blockhouse

Doddrige's Fort

Rice's Fort

Catfish Camp
(Washington, PA)

Redstone
Old Fort
(Brownsville, PA)

OHIO RIVER

Short Creek

Shepherd's Fort
Middle Wheeling Ck.

Site of Foreman's
Massacre

The Narrows

Wheeling Creek

Ohio County (1776)
Marshall County (1835)

Washington County
PA

Grave Creek
Blockhouse

Ryerson's
Station

Greene County
PA

WESTERN VIRGINA

Captina Creek

Revolutionary Era
FORTS and BLOCKHOUSES
In the Upper Ohio Valley
1775 - 1795

N

(Fort Bollings not located)

© 2009 - Michael E. Nogay
Graphics by Dennis R. Jones

CHAPTER VII

THE STORY OF JOHN STRUTHERS

The American Revolutionary War pension applications in the National Archives contain a treasure trove of information in its 80,000 files. In 1832, when men who had fought during the revolutionary years were in their seventies and eighties, Congress passed a pension act providing benefits to those who had served for at least six months. An elderly soldier would go to a courthouse clerk, a lawyer, or a pension agent and relate his revolutionary war service in the form of a sworn, written affidavit in the hopes of being granted a pension. Despite the passage of over 50 years from the date of service, many of the applications contain extraordinary details of the revolutionary period.

In 1980, John C. Dann of The Clements Library at the University of Michigan edited a book* containing the narrative portions (or oral history) of 79 Revolutionary War-era pension applications. One in particular, that of John Struthers (1759-1845), contains an amazing tale of frontier Indian forts in the Upper Ohio Valley and covers precisely the time and locale detailed in this book. This same affidavit has also been published in *Documents to Accompany America's History*.**

Originally from Maryland, Struthers migrated with his father and family to Washington County, Pennsylvania in 1773. In May of

---

*John C. Dann, editor, *The Revolution Remembered, Eyewitness Accounts of the War for Independence* (University of Chicago Press: 1980) 251-258. Unfortunately, the index incorrectly lists Holliday's Cove as located in Pennsylvania, rather than Virginia, apparently confusing it with another fort in Hollidaysburg, PA.

**Melvin Yazawa, *Documents to Accompany America's History*, Fifth Edition, vol. 1 (Bedford/St. Martin's: 2004) 135-137.

1776, at the age of 16, Struthers joined the Virginia militia at Ft. Pitt. The following year, Struthers again volunteered:

> The summer of 1777 was a season of great alarm, and the whole settlement from Ft. Pitt to Kentucky was broken up. A number of families assembled at the house of my father in order to erect a fort, but hearing that families had collected at Hoagland's [see map] and Beelor's, [see map] eight or ten miles nearer to the Ohio, for the same purpose, they only repaired the cabins as well as they could to resist an attack and remained in them during the summer. The others went on and built forts.
>
> It was early resolved to raise a small company of volunteers to act as spies and wood rangers. Capt. James Scott, a brave and experienced officer, offered his services and appointed a place of rendezvous, and in a few days had upwards of twenty, of whom I was one, enrolled and ready to march with as much provision as we could conveniently carry. We started about the first of May, as nearly as I can now state, and I state it accordingly to be on that day. The country traversed was from a few miles below Ft. Pitt, down the Ohio, crossing Raccoon Creek, Traver's and Tomlinson's Runs, Cross Creek, King's and Heoman's (Harmon's) creeks [see map], near their junction with the Ohio, passing on our way down Reardon's and Holliday's stations [see map] where we occasionally drew provisions.
>
> From Holliday's Cove, we traversed the country backward and forward, carefully watching the Indian warpaths until we arrived at some one of the forts or stations on the headwaters of some of the streams above mentioned, in the vicinity of which most of our company resided, where we remained a day or two to get washing and mending done and a recruit of provisions, and at every station would spend an hour or two in the exercise of the tomahawk and rifle, not only for our own improvement in the use of these weapons of warfare but also to alarm the savages if they should be lurking in the neighborhood.

In the latter part of the season, the alarm was still kept up and increased by the attack (as was reported at the time) of two or three hundred Indians on Wheeling Fort [Ft. Henry], and in this stage of alarm many others volunteered to protect the frontier, and so effectually was the country scoured from Holliday's Cove to Fort Pitt, that, though we had no triumphs in battle to record nor defeats to lament, yet not an individual was massacred by the savages in that region during this year. I ask credit for six months only during this season, that is, from the first of May till in November, when the cold weather forced the Indians to return to their towns. And I am quite confident that I served at least six months this year...

Early in the spring of 1780 intelligence was received, I do not remember how, that a large body of Indians were on their march to devastate the whole country from Wheeling to Fort Pitt. This news was either not believed or at least not heeded until a party of them, crossing below Wheeling, had penetrated nearly halfway from the Ohio to Catfish Camp, now the seat of justice for Washington County, Pennsylvania.

They had taken a number of prisoners, but becoming alarmed, speedily retraced their steps to the Ohio and murdered all their male prisoners on the way. The main body of those who were expected to have ravaged Raccoon settlement, it was supposed, never crossed the Ohio, but sent two of their warriors to reconnoiter, who, approaching Dillow's Fort [see map] late in the evening, spied two boys at play and tomahawked and scalped them within two hundred yards of the fort and escaped.

Unfortunately, despite his service in the Upper Ohio Valley and as a volunteer in 1779 with General McIntosh's campaign to Fort Laurens on the Tuscarawas River in Ohio, the federal government denied Struthers a veteran's pension. Struthers, in the closing remarks of his application, takes aim at the notion that the regular or Continental troops were superior to the volunteer militia along the Ohio River outposts:

The regular soldier performs only during the summer and then retires to winter quarters, receiving pay and clothing and rations for the whole year. The volunteers, to whom I belonged, performed at least an equal amount of service and retired home during the winter, not receiving either pay or rations and not even clothing for any part of the time, with the trifling exceptions of a little flour obtained now and then at the posts, or stations, and furnishing their own ammunition. Justice therefore requires that these volunteers, on applying for pensions, should have their time calculated in the same rule as the regulars.

The few regulars stationed along the Ohio, from Pitt to Wheeling, and I here speak of them only, the only reliance placed on them was to defend the forts should they be attacked. Indeed, it was admitted by everyone at the time that the only security of the people along the river and adjacent settlements was the vigilance of the volunteers in watching their crossing places and warpaths and ferreting them out of their lurking places near the stations, and that by their means, principally, was the settlement saved from savage vengeances. [1]

Struthers also mentions Andrew Poe's fight with Indians who had kidnapped a man named "Jackson" in March 1782. Struthers claimed that the Indian who survived the rescue effort (Scotash), "was often at Pittsburgh after the peace [and] would show his wound and exalt in his dexterity in hiding himself." [See pages 57-60 herein.]

Struthers lived in Washington County, Pennsylvania until 1798, then moved to Trumbull County, Ohio, where he died in 1845 at the age of 86.

CHAPTER VIII

SIMON GIRTY, A MAN BETWEEN

He has been called an "outlaw," the "white savage," a "famous traitor," and a "monster" in biographies. Even a relative seeking to vindicate him called him "the most notorious character of the American Revolution." J.H. Newton, in 1879, wrote:

> No other country or age ever produced perhaps so brutal, depraved and wicked a wretch as Simon Girty. He was sagacious and brave; but his sagacity and bravery only made him a greater monster of cruelty. [1]

In a period of American history that gave us Benedict Arnold and frontiersmen who routinely killed women and children, what deeds of Simon Girty burn so dark more than 200 years later?

Girty's mere presence as an Indian ally on July 11, 1782, while Colonel William Crawford was burned alive at the stake and then beheaded, would have been enough to secure his place in infamy. But when two eyewitnesses to the torture of Crawford, Dr. John Knight and John Slover, escaped their Delaware captors and reported the incident, Girty's vilification was sealed.

In the days before the internet and cable news networks, imagine how difficult it would have been to become a legend in your own time. Those who became household names on the Ohio frontier, such as Daniel Boone, Betty Zane, and Captain Samuel Brady, typically did so by heroic acts so great that they stood out in a time where bravery was an everyday occurrence. Girty gained notoriety in precisely the opposite fashion.

Born in Pennsylvania in 1741, Simon Girty and his brothers, James and George, were captured in 1755 by Seneca Indians during the French and Indian War. Already a teenager, Girty was raised to manhood in his three years of captivity by the Indians and adopted many of their customs. Girty was "released" around 1759, and it appeared he would live the life of an itinerate farmer. According to some authorities, such a release from captivity was unusual. The Wyandot tribe in Ohio, for instance, accepted their "adopted" children as their own, and expected the captive to embrace tribal life and never attempt to escape. Those who did attempt to flee and were captured could be burned alive or scalped as an example to others.

After his own release, brother George (1745-1811) became an interpreter and trader, and later allied himself with the Shawnee and lived for a time among Captain Pipe and the Delaware. Meanwhile, brother James (1743-1817) also became an ally of the Shawnee and the British. James is said to have been with the Indian party that attacked Fort Henry in Wheeling. [2]

The 1770s was a decade in which one's allegiance to either Britain, America or the Indian nations was a life or death decision. Like others raised within two cultures, Simon Girty was truly a "man between." Serving first as interpreter for the British at Fort Dunmore (soon to be renamed Fort Pitt), Girty later acted as a scout for the crown, and then for the Americans.

At the outbreak of the Revolution in 1775, Girty assisted the colonists in their negotiations with the Indian nations. By the fall of 1777, however, Girty had been dismissed from the service of the Americans. He was subsequently tried and acquitted of treason, allegedly for having conspired to aid the British in seizing Fort Pitt.

Apparently with no other path open to him, Girty joined forces with the British in Detroit in 1778. Over the next five years, Girty would facilitate Indian attacks on numerous white settlements. Although dismissed by contemporary historians, Girty—like his brother James-- was even said, by at least one witness, to have led the first siege against Ft. Henry in Wheeling in 1777. [3]

The ill-fated campaign of Col. William Crawford against the Wyandot in Ohio began with a mustering of 480 soldiers on May 25, 1782, just below Holliday's Cove Fort at Mingo Bottom. As was the militia tradition, an election of officers by all the soldiers was held and, "through the influence of General Irvine," Crawford was elected commander of the expedition over Col. David Williamson by a margin of only five votes. With "apparent reluctance" Crawford accepted the vote of the troops to be their commander.

Marching along Williamson's Trail across the Ohio country, Crawford's army soon arrived at Sandusky. There, subjected to sporadic sniping, soldiers began deserting in a confused retreat. Crawford sought to locate his missing son, John, and was soon separated from the main force. Falling in with other retreating soldiers and the corps' doctor, John Knight, Col. Crawford and the physician were subsequently captured and marched off to a Wyandot town for execution. [4]

Crawford, "naked and shackled, his hands secured to a nearby tree by a short length of rope," was subjected to grotesque torture by his Delaware captors. Soon his ears were cut off and red-hot tips of smoldering branches were pressed into his chest, face, and groin. The Indians shot him at point blank range with their muskets. This was all done in the presence of Simon Girty.

> Overcome by agony, Crawford cried out, "Girty! Girty! For God's sake, Girty, shoot me through the heart." After a moment of introspection, Girty arose from his seat by the fire and strode to where Crawford lay sobbing. "I cannot," Girty replied. "As you can see, I have no gun."

Girty then turned away from Crawford and grinned and laughed for the Indians. Encouraged, his captors scalped Crawford's hair from his skull and threw what remained of his body into the raging fire. [5]

The frontier was rife with white children who had been captured and raised by the Indians. Thomas McKee had been captured by the Shawnee and condemned to death, only to be saved by a Shawnee girl whom he later married. McKee thereafter became a successful trader between the Indians and settlers. Another trader, Conrad Weiser, is said to have been voluntarily given over to the Mohawk tribe in New York by his father who was anxious for his son to "learn their customs and language." Daniel Boone, Simon Kenton, Lewis Wetzel and Thomas Edgington had all been held captive by Indians at various times but returned to the frontier to become heroes. The admittedly harrowing experience of being kidnapped at the hands of Indians thus cannot excuse acts of depravity later in Girty's life. [6]

Nonetheless, another side of Girty, a more humane and decent side, has only recently begun to receive a hearing through the pens of more sympathetic biographers.

One well-documented story from 1777 reflects well on Girty. Simon Kenton was one of the era's greatest frontiersmen and George Rogers Clark's favorite scout. It was Kenton who organized a party of 200 men in 1789 to demand the release of another frontier hero, Lewis Wetzel, when Wetzel had been sentenced to hang for the killing of an allied Indian.

Twelve years earlier, however, it was Kenton who was the captive of the Shawnee, after having been captured in Kentucky while attempting to steal Indian horses. The sentence of death by burning at the stake had been pronounced on Kenton.

Entering the Shawnee village with a band of Wyandot, Simon Girty had recognized Kenton, a friend from earlier days. In a biography of Kenton written by a relative, Edna Kenton, in 1926, Girty is said to have approached the prisoner and "flung his arms around" Kenton and "cried like a child." Girty then made an impassioned speech to the Indians in their native tongue, telling them "that if they ever meant to do him a favor they must do it now." A long debate ensued between Girty and two Shawnee war captains who wanted Kenton to burn. Girty's oratory prevailed and Kenton was spared a gruesome death. [7]

That Girty was a hunted man in the Ohio Valley shortly after saving Kenton and even before the Crawford torture is without question. In the summer of 1779, Col. Daniel Brodhead at Ft. Pitt had sent his best ranger, Captain Samuel Brady, along with a team led by the noted Indian scout, John Montour, to Holliday's Cove Fort in pursuit of Girty who was said to be "lurking (there) with seven Mingo Indians." [8]

Girty's most recent biographer, Phillip W. Hoffman, also paints a more sympathetic portrait of the man he calls, paradoxically, the "turncoat hero." Hoffman argues that Girty actually sought to comfort Crawford while the colonel was in captivity in the days before his death. Girty allegedly told Crawford that his nephew, William Crawford, and his son-in-law, William Harrison (both of whom had also been captured) were safe and unharmed, despite the fact that both had already been put to death by the Shawnee, as a way of comforting the colonel. When Girty told Crawford that the Delaware blamed him for the Gnadenhutten massacre of the Christian Moravian Indians,

> Crawford reacted as though he had been slapped. He adamantly denied participating in any way in that tragedy...

Elizabeth Turner told Dr. Draper in an interview that she was present when Girty met with Crawford in captivity. Girty, Turner said, suggested an escape plan, but Crawford had "no heart" for such a mission. Nevertheless, Turner recalled, Girty promised Crawford he would do all he could to save him.

The trial of Crawford commenced before a council of chiefs. Girty acted as an interpreter for Crawford, who vehemently denied any involvement in the Gnadenhutten killings. The chiefs nonetheless condemned Crawford to death.

Joseph Jackson, a white man living with the Shawnee, later reported that Girty subsequently told him he "got on his knees and begged" the council to spare Crawford, all to no avail. Girty's daughter, some eight decades after Crawford's execution, told Dr. Draper that when Crawford asked to be shot, Girty had replied that it was Indian custom that no one could interfere with a prisoner condemned to death without risking death himself (ignoring for a moment that Girty had successfully begged for the life of Simon Kenton in 1777). But, if Girty's daughter was right, what was he to do? He was clearly a man caught between two warring cultures.

When Dr. Knight managed his escape to Ft. Pitt and related his story to Gen. Irvine, the latter wrote on July 11, 1782, to George Washington that "... the colonel (Crawford) begged Girty to shoot him, but he paid no regard to the request."

As the news of Crawford's torturous death swept the frontier it "was sensationalized in American newspapers." Crawford was, after all, a top ranking American soldier.

> Girty's supposed participation in the victim's execution served as a dark indictment from which his reputation would never recover. [9]

Girty engaged in his last battle against the settlers in 1791 at the headwaters of the Wabash River, in present-day Mercer County, Ohio, assisting with the devastating Indian defeat of Maj. Gen. Arthur St. Clair and the deaths of over 800 soldiers. This defeat was said to have enraged Gen. George Washington and in turn led to an "upsurge of attacks in the Ohio River Valley from above Wheeling all the way down to the mouth of the Ohio."

After continuing to fight alongside the Indians in their defense of the Ohio country, Girty became a trader for several years before retiring far away from the Ohio Valley in Detroit. There he lived comfortably on a pension paid by the Indian Department of the British government.

Girty was described in 1813 by a man who knew him as "five feet six or seven inches (in height) broad across the chest; strong, round, compact limbs, and of fair complexion."[10]

Escaping capture until his death in 1818 at the age of 77, Girty was given a full military funeral by the British government at Fort Malden on the Detroit River in Canada. [11]

Lewis Wetzel admitted murdering, without provocation and in cold blood, an Indian chief whom an American general described as one of the finest men he knew. After being set free without punishment, Wetzel was again jailed for counterfeiting. Yet, Wetzel was a hero on the frontier. His friends and acquaintances thought so much of him that they were willing to risk their lives to prevent his arrest by federal troops at Mingo Bottom. Meanwhile, Girty was demonized.

In his *History of the Backwoods* published in 1843, A.W. Patterson wrote that he personally interviewed three Western Pennsylvanians who actually knew Simon Girty. It was the consensus of these men that "Girty, although bad enough, had an undue share of infamy heaped upon him, and often had the curses of his countrymen for acts he knew nothing of." He was, of course, a friend and ally of the enemy in the eyes of his fellow frontiersmen.

Simon Girty was never given much quarter by most writers of the period. An American born white man, Girty had sided with the enemy—first the British and then the Indians—and, on the frontier of the Ohio Valley, there was no place for a man between.

CHAPTER IX

BIG JOHN WETZEL'S SONS

Big John Wetzel and his wife Mary built their homestead on Wheeling Creek, far enough from Ft. Henry that the family had to always be on the alert. They had five sons who grew to be frontier legends: Martin, born in 1757; George, born in 1761; Lewis, born in 1763; Jacob, born in 1765; and Little John, born in 1770. The family surname had been derived from craftsmen who sharpened tools to a fine cutting edge (Whetsel, like "wet stone), and that was exactly how Big John raised his boys. [1]

The most famous of the siblings, Lewis, was to the Ohio Valley what Daniel Boone was to Kentucky. Known for his uncanny ability to load a flintlock rifle while being pursued, Lewis is said to have killed over 70 Indians in his lifetime. In fact, on the frontier, only Simon Kenton was judged to have had near the same ability as Lewis Wetzel to reload fast enough on the run to surprise any pursuer.

Lewis Wetzel never married and had a hankering to go places. He spent five years jailed in New Orleans late in life, but unlike other rogues such as Samuel Mason and Simon Girty, he was beloved by his fellow frontiersmen.

In 1776, when he was only 13, Lewis and his brother, Jacob, were abducted by Indians as they worked on the family farm near Shepherd's Fort. Within days, the boys had escaped their Wyandot captors, stealing a rifle in the process and safely crossing the Ohio on their return. The legend that was Lewis Wetzel had begun.

The following year, older brother Martin was in Captain Sam Mason's company when Ft. Henry was attacked. Cut off from the fort while on patrol, Martin managed his way back to safety. A few weeks later, Martin Wetzel used another of his nine lives as he miraculously survived the massacre of Captain Foreman's company at The Narrows in present-day Marshall County when he smelled an ambush and took a more circuitous route.

The second oldest of the Wetzel boys, George, was killed by Indians in 1782, at the tender age of 20. He had been on a hunting trip with his father, brother Lewis, and two other friends along the Ohio. The party was attacked and George was struck down. His father and brother temporarily interred George's body on an island in the Ohio River and returned days later with a party from Wheeling to bring the young man's remains home to Ohio County. [2]

That same year Lewis Wetzel and John Mills, the latter having just returned from Col. Crawford's disastrous mission to Sandusky, were attacked by a band of 40 to 50 Indians near what is now St. Clairsville, Ohio. The two men had brought along a 15-year-old friend, John Davis, while they sought to retrieve Mills' runaway horse. Over 60 years later, a significantly older John Davis recalled the story for the Barnesville (Ohio) *Enterprise* in 1845.

Davis told the newspaper of Lewis Wetzel's heroics that day in saving his life with no fear for his own. Mills had been shot in the ankle, captured and scalped. Wetzel, with no time to mourn his friend, led young Davis through the woods, loading and reloading on the run, all the while keeping their pursuers at bay. [3]

As Gen. "Mad" Anthony Wayne was defeating the Wyandot at Fallen Timber in 1794, Lewis Wetzel and John Davis, now 29, were together again near Dillow's Fort at the headwaters of Raccoon Creek [see map]. It seems a certain Michael Forshay, not realizing he was in the company of the great Lewis Wetzel, bragged that no man could "come in on him when he was in the woods." Up to the challenge, Wetzel bet a round of liquor that he could sneak up on Forshay and tap him on the shoulder before Forshay could notice him. Like a "ghost," according Davis, Wetzel used his stealth to creep in on Forshay on "dry leaves" and grab his shoulder. It was a skill that allowed Wetzel to survive in arguably the most dangerous day-to-day environment ever known on this continent.

Lewis Wetzel killed Indians without remorse, quietly, brutally, with malice aforethought, taking a scalp just to receive the bounty or the moment's admiration from his fellow frontiersmen. It was a nauseous circle of hatred and retribution killing, with neither the Indians nor the invading white settlers ever able to capture the moral high ground.

An eye for an eye; your brother for mine. Two starving tribes fighting for the last scrap of food. The frontiersmen, like soldiers in other wars who faced such brutality, dehumanized the opposition as "savages," unworthy of any mercy. The Indians replied in kind. It was what it was, and men like Lewis Wetzel, who could set conscience aside, thrived.

Not only in the heat of battle or in the defense of himself or others did Lewis Wetzel kill Indians. He killed Chief Killbuck while the warrior was helplessly in captivity at Ft. Henry in 1781. On other occasions he stabbed Indians in their sleep or killed them unsuspectedly by sniper fire during times of peace. [4]

The cycle of hatred finally caught up to Lewis Wetzel. An Indian, who went by the curious name of "George Washington," and who was allied with General Josiah Harmar, was found murdered. When confronted with the murder, Lewis Wetzel "admitted without hesitation" that it was he who had shot the man. George Washington's birth name had been QueYshaw-say, and he was a Delaware chief and Indian peace emissary. He was described by Gen. Harmar in a letter to Secretary of War Henry Knox as "...a trusty confidential Indian... there is not a better Indian to be found." Gen. Harmar, then stationed in Marietta on the Ohio, decided enough was enough. He wanted Wetzel "hanged up immediately without trial," but instead ordered the frontier hero jailed . [5]

It was a gamble on the part of Harmar. No white jury on the frontier would ever believe a white man could "murder" an Indian in the criminal sense of the word. Indians were considered by most as non-human, a natural enemy who had to be eradicated. Jailed and shackled for days, Wetzel asked for the right to exercise, as he "could not live much longer if he was not permitted some room to walk about." Wetzel had, in fact, earlier offered to run the gauntlet, Indian style, facing tomahawks rather than "be hung like a dog." Harmar denied the gauntlet request, but ordered Wetzel's jailers to "knock off his iron fetters" and allow him time to stretch his legs under close guard. As anyone, perhaps even Gen. Harmar, could imagine, Wetzel escaped. [6]

Angered by the escape, Gen. Harmar offered a large reward for Wetzel's capture. A short while later, in the fall of 1788, Wetzel could not resist competing in a shooting competition being held at Mingo Bottom, near present-day Steubenville. Learning of Wetzel's whereabouts, Gen. Harmar dispatched troops to secure the fugitive's arrest. The local population had a different idea, however.

A mob formed, and the federal troops, under the command of Captain Jacob Kingsbury, were forced to back down. The intervention of Maj. William McMahon, the commander of Shepherd's Fort, across the Ohio in Virginia, caused calmer heads to prevail. The arresting troops, after all, had come to a place where the Ohio Valley's best marksmen had congregated. The odds were in Wetzel's favor; his fellow shooting competitors felt like he did about Indians.

Stationed down the Ohio now, at Cincinnati, Gen. Harmar increased the reward for the capture of Lewis Wetzel. Soon federal troops captured the fugitive in Kentucky. The great outpouring of support for Wetzel by his fellow settlers eventually caused Gen. Harmar to back down and release him. The murder of the Indian known as George Washington went forever unpunished. [7]

Lewis Wetzel was soon to have another opportunity to place his name among the nation's bravest frontiersmen. A women by the name of Rose Forester was kidnapped by Indians near Captina Creek. A stirring rescue by Lewis Wetzel of the damsel was immortalized in a romantic book about the adventure published in 1861 by the novelist Emerson Bennett titled, *Forest Rose*. Betty Zane had Zane Grey to immortalize her; likewise Lewis Wetzel had his biographer. The legend grew, even years after his death.

The West Virginia Division of Culture and History republished online an 1837 story about Lewis Wetzel which appeared in a publication called *The Casket*. Even in view of the romanticism of the times , the language used to describe Wetzel is fawning, considering, according to Eckert's calculations, Lewis was still alive until his death in1839.

*The Casket** prose included the following:

His form was erect, and (he was) very muscular, and possessed of great bodily strength…(Wetzel) was a man of frankness, skill and fine personal appearance.

Another publication of the West Virginia Division of Culture and History, written by George Carroll in 1991, relied upon interviews taken by Dr. Lyman Draper 150 years earlier of men who actually knew Lewis Wetzel. An individual named Christian Cackler told Draper that Wetzel was "a man about six feet and well-proportioned, rather raw boned and active, dark and swarthy. I have seen Indians I thought [were] as white as he was."

Lewis Bonnett, Jr., the son of a militia captain who had served with Martin Wetzel , recalled Lewis Wetzel as "possessing very muscular arms and shoulders with well-proportioned legs and smallish feet, braided hair carefully knotted around his shoulders which reached nearly to his calves when combed out, extremely piercing black eyes from which he wore silk tassels and other ornaments."[8]

Self-inflicted trouble followed Wetzel as he moved restlessly across the frontier. From Kentucky he migrated by way of the Natchez Trail in 1808 to New Orleans. In Louisiana, Wetzel is said to have unknowingly passed a counterfeit bill that had been given to him days earlier in exchange for pelts. He was jailed and then released and began living with a "Spaniard" and his family. Lewis and the Spaniard were soon arrested for counterfeiting pewter coins. Wetzel protested his innocence, but was jailed for a period of over five years.

According to Clarence B. Allman, a distant relative who wrote *The Life and Times of Lewis Wetzel* in 1931, Wetzel was finally released from jail when a trader who was originally from Pennsylvania, John Miner, faked the death of Wetzel and smuggled him out of the prison in a coffin which was later interred empty.

Upon his escape, Lewis Wetzel is said to have exacted revenge on the counterfeiter who had caused his imprisonment. This assertion,

---

The Casket article indicates Wetzel died some time after "the peace of 1795," after he had moved to new frontiers on the Mississippi. The author of the article might not have known Wetzel was still alive and living in Texas at that time. C.B. Allman reported that the Texas Historical Association believed Lewis Wetzel died in Texas in 1830.

perhaps mere bravado by a biographer, suggests a rage in Wetzel that bespeaks his innocence.

By most accounts, Wetzel continued his relentless reign of murder against the Indians until his death. Eckert even tells a story of Wetzel acting as a sniper, killing Indians who were harmless and merely passing by.

Perhaps it was the pecuniary gain of the bounty on Indian scalps that encouraged Wetzel to act out his hatred. There was the "booty," as well. Dead Indians could be swiftly relieved of their earthly possessions without the objection of bystanders.

The spoils from a fortunate raid could be of considerable value by frontier standards. Indian trinkets were frequently silver, and often became a circulating medium of exchange in frontier trading communities, which were chronically short of hard cash. So accustomed to adventure and the resulting spoils were some elements of both the Indian and white populations, that they mutually resisted efforts at peace settlements. [9]

Amazingly, Lewis Wetzel lived to the ripe old age of 75, and died in 1839 in Austin, Texas, where he was buried, although he was said to have been re-interred in Marshall County, West Virginia in 1942. [10]

Meanwhile, Martin Wetzel had married and raised a family on Wheeling Creek. He died in 1812 at the age of 55. After serving as a Justice of the Peace in Ohio County, Jacob Wetzel fell on hard financial times and moved his family to Indiana in 1807. Jacob died there in 1833 at the age of 67. Young John worked as an elk hunter near present-day Charleston, West Virginia; he died in 1815 at the age of 45.

Against all odds, Lewis Wetzel, the most daring and reckless of Big John's five sons had outlived them all. [11]

CHAPTER X

THE PENNSYLVANIA RIFLE
AND OTHER WEAPONRY

Skilled craftsmen who apprenticed in the trade guilds of Europe began migrating to America in the middle part of the 1700s. These men in turn trained others in such crafts as silversmithing, watch making, locksmithing and gun making.

Men such George Snyder and Jonathan Meek used their watch making skills to cut gears, which in turn led to the handmade production of the first "multiplying" fishing reels in America as early as 1813. With this innovation, one turn of the crank handle resulted in multiple turns of the line spool, which in turn resulted in faster and more leveraged retrieval of the fishing line.

Since the vast majority of these reel makers lived near Frankfort, Kentucky, the term "Kentucky reel" is today synonymous with the finest of early craftsmanship and collectability. In fact, these Kentucky craftsmen were so certain of the quality of their product that they refused to even apply for patent protection. Benjamin Meek, brother of Jonathan, explained his indifference to obtaining a patent to protect his work product:

> If any man can produce a reel equal to mine, he is welcome to all the money he can make from it. [1]

Unfortunately, the famous "Kentucky rifle" acquired its title in a slightly different manner, via a popular song, to be exact.

The birthplace of quality rifle making in America is generally accepted to be Lancaster County, Pennsylvania, not the Bluegrass

State. Martin Meylin, also spelled Meillin (1670-1749), a gunsmith born in Switzerland, was likely the first in a long line of Pennsylvania rifle makers who supplied this unique long-range weapon to hunters and militiamen. The Commonwealth of Pennsylvania has recognized Meylin as the first gunsmith in Lancaster County.

However, as Professor James B. Whisker notes in his classic treatise, *Arms Makers of Colonial America*,* it is controversial to call Meylin the "father" of the Pennsylvania-Kentucky rifle; there appears to be some evidence that Meylin was only a blacksmith whose son-in-law, Joshua Baker, actually owned the gunsmith tools in his estate inventory.

Whoever was first, these talented Pennsylvania gunsmiths took the German "jaeger" version of the rifle (30 inch barrel, .60 caliber ball) and refined it into a more accurate gun with a longer 40 to 48 inch barrel and a smaller .50 caliber ball which would carry for greater distances and conserve precious lead.

Both the old European musket and the new "Pennsylvania" rifle still relied on the tried and tested "flintlock" firing system. When the flintlock gun was fired, the "cock" holding a flint in its jaws would swing in an arc, scraping the flint on hardened steel (known as the "frizzen"), thus producing a shower of sparks. This movement also forces the frizzen forward, revealing a "flash pan" filled with priming powder. The sparks ignite the powder which in turn ignites the main powder charge in the barrel which expels the ball. This entire process takes place in a fraction of a second.

The obvious downside to the flintlock system was the exposure of the priming powder and the flint to the elements. A moist priming charge will not ignite. The solution to the problem over time was the "percussion" lock. This system uses a percussion "cap" to replace the flint and frizzen. The hammer of the gun falls directly on the cap, which in turn ignites the fulminate and the resulting flame is directed through a "flash hole" and into the main charge in the barrel.

A Scottish minister obtained the first patent for the percussion system in 1807, apparently not being of same mindset as Benjamin Meek. [2]

---

* The author is proud to note than Dr. Whisker was one of his political science professors at West Virginia University in the late 1970s.

In Berks County, Pennsylvania, tax records reveal gunsmiths such as Wolfgang Hacka and William Graeff plying their trade as early as 1758. The Pennsylvania long guns of this period were often aesthetically beautiful—graceful curly maple stocks, brass mountings and patch boxes decorated with silver or bone inlays. The austerity of the frontier gave way to the pride an owner felt when he became the recipient of what would likely be the finest example of material craftsmanship he might ever possess.

The term "Kentucky rifle" entered the American lexicon following the War of 1812 when a popular song, "The Hunters of Kentucky," celebrated the victory of Andrew Jackson at the Battle of New Orleans. Despite the fact the vast majority of long rifles made in America during the so-called "Golden Age" of rifle making (1775 to 1825) were actually crafted in Pennsylvania, the name stuck.

Marksmanship with the Pennsylvania rifle was a much admired trait on the frontier, for reasons that started and ended with life and death. Not only was the rifle used for protection from the Indians, hunting wild game was a daily rite of survival. The lighter load and longer barrel gave hunters greater range to down their prey. Of course, whether a rifle had a "smooth" bore or one that was "rifled" also greatly affected its accuracy. Rifling the inside of a gun barrel causes the projectile to rotate like a quarterback throwing a football spiral which in turn allows the shot to fly more accurately.

Shooting competitions were a favorite pastime. When Gen. "Mad" Anthony Wayne was mustering his army of 2,500 men in 1793 in anticipation of his Ohio campaign against the Wyandot, they camped overnight in Wellsburg (WV). Captain Sam Brady told Gen. Wayne "that any two of his Rangers could outshoot a whole 100 of whatever men Wayne chose from his army." Shooting from a distance of 250 feet at a 20-inch target carved into a tree, Wayne selected his 100 shooters and Brady his two marksmen. Needless to say, Brady's Rangers won a keg of rum that day. [3] It was also at a shooting competition at nearby Mingo Bottom that the armed contestants backed down federal troops that had come to arrest Lewis Wetzel for murder in 1788.

As John Struthers wrote in his Revolutionary War pension application:

...at every station we would spend an hour or two in the exercise of the tomahawk and rifle, not only for our own improvement in the use of these weapons of warfare but also to alarm the savages if they should be lurking in the neighborhood.

By the mid-1700s the Indians had begun to give up the bow and arrow in favor of the rifle. The Indians traded land and fur for guns and gunpowder. Not only did guns enable the tribes to "kill bear, bison, elk, moose and other large animals at will," but also "guns had become an absolute necessity in war." [4]

Times had changed the weaponry on the Ohio frontier.

THE TOMAHAWK AND SCALPING KNIFE

Adaptation is the key to survival in any environment. The frontiersmen soon found out the usefulness of a weapon that never misfired and was always loaded. Their enemy relied on the tomahawk and so would they.

The tomahawk was used to mark boundaries and take scalps. It was a weapon for close combat and, once the art of tomahawk throwing was mastered, it could also be useful at a distance, as well. It was the backup weapon of choice.

Every man who served in that country can attest the fact, that the Kentuckians invariably carried the tomahawk and scalping knife into action, and are dexterous in using them. [5]

Throwing the tomahawk was a skill learned at a young age by boys on the frontier. The 'hawk would make a certain number of revolutions, depending on its length, over a given distance.

Say in five steps it will strike with the edge, the handle downwards; at the distance of seven and a half, it will strike with the edge, the handle upwards, and so on. A little experience enabled the boy to measure the distance with his eye, when walking through the woods, and strike a tree with his tomahawk in any way he chose. [6]

According to Dr. Doddridge, the "scalping knife" was carried in a leather sheath "suspended to the belt of the hunting shirt" of many frontiersmen. It was such a mainstay on the frontier that it was even used as an eating utensil. [7] One Indian, killed in 1778 in present-day West Virginia by Levi Morgan, had in his possession, "an elegant gun, considerable ammunition, a tomahawk and scalping knife…" [8]

By the time the Ohio Valley was being settled, use of the bow and arrow was on the decline by the Indians, who traded with the British for rifles or muskets or had been given guns while allies of Britain or France during the French and Indian War. Wrote Doddridge: "…I much doubt whether any of the present tribes of Indians could make much use of the flint arrow heads which must have been so generally used by their forefathers…fire arms, wherever they can be obtained, soon put an end to the use of the bow and arrow." [9]

The arrowheads that are still found throughout fields and streams in the Ohio Valley are likely the products of hunters and warriors of a slightly earlier era than the Revolutionary period.

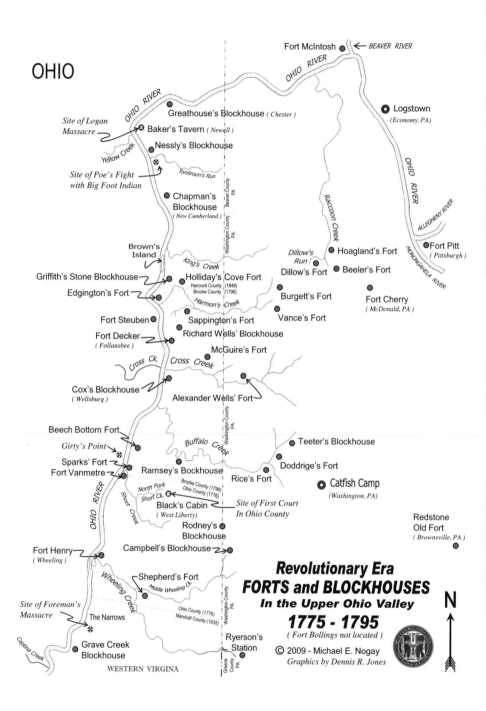

OHIO

Fort McIntosh ●◖ ← *BEAVER RIVER*

OHIO RIVER

OHIO RIVER

Logstown ●
(Economy, PA)

Greathouse's Blockhouse *(Chester)*

Site of Logan Massacre

Baker's Tavern *(Newell)*

Nessly's Blockhouse ●

Yellow Creek

Site of Poe's Fight with Big Foot Indian

Tomlinson's Run

Chapman's ● Blockhouse
(New Cumberland)

Beaver County PA

OHIO RIVER

ALLEGHENY RIVER

Raccoon Creek

Brown's Island

King's Creek

Dillow's Run

Hoagland's Fort ●

● Fort Pitt
(Pittsburgh)

Griffith's Stone Blockhouse

Holliday's Cove Fort
Hancock County (1848)
Brooke County (1796)

Dillow's Fort ●

Beeler's Fort ●

MONONGAHELA RIVER

Edgington's Fort

Harmon's Creek

Burgett's Fort ●

Fort Cherry
(McDonald, PA)

Fort Steuben ●

Sappington's Fort ●

Vance's Fort ●

Fort Decker
(Follansbee)

Richard Wells' Blockhouse ●

McGuire's Fort ●

Cross Ck. *Cross Creek*

Cox's Blockhouse
(Wellsburg)

Alexander Wells' Fort

Beech Bottom Fort

Washington County PA

Girty's Point

Buffalo Creek

Teeter's Blockhouse ●

Sparks' Fort
Fort Vanmetre

Ramsey's Bockhouse ●

Doddrige's Fort ●

North Fork Brooke County (1796)
Short Ck. ✖ Ohio County (1776)

Rice's Fort ●

Catfish Camp ◉
(Washington, PA)

OHIO RIVER

Short Creek

Black's Cabin
(West Liberty)

Site of First Court In Ohio County

Redstone Old Fort
(Brownsville, PA)
●

Rodney's ● Blockhouse

Fort Henry
(Wheeling)

Campbell's Blockhouse

Shepherd's Fort
Middle Wheeling Ck.

Ohio County (1776)
Marshall County (1835)

Washington County PA

Revolutionary Era
FORTS and BLOCKHOUSES
In the Upper Ohio Valley
1775 - 1795

N ↑

Site of Foreman's Massacre

The Narrows

Ryerson's Station

(Fort Bollings not located)

Carolina Creek

Grave Creek Blockhouse ●

© 2009 - Michael E. Nogay
Graphics by Dennis R. Jones

Greene County PA

WESTERN VIRGINA

- 112 -

CONCLUSION

A BROKEN WILDERNESS

In 1768 the idea that a white settler would cross the Ohio River was foolhardy.

Travelers journeying downstream wrote of an "Indian coast" and a "Virginia shore" as if an ocean's expanse rather than a few hundred yards separated the banks of the river. [1]

A generation of brave and murderous frontiersmen later, things had changed .

Meriwether Lewis (1774-1809), the great explorer who had been President Thomas Jefferson's personal secretary, stopped in "Stewbenville" on his way down the mighty Ohio River in 1803, and found the settlement to be a "small, well-built, thriving place… five years since it was a wilderness." Two days later, upon arriving in Wheeling, he noted "a pretty considerable village of fifty houses." [2]

Below Wheeling, the Ohio River valley was so lush with wild game that Lewis was able to use his Newfoundland dog to fetch migrating squirrels literally swimming across the water. Lewis fried them; "they were fat and a pleasant food." Floating down the Ohio, he noted:

The banks were lined with hardwoods, deep green, enclosing. All the sounds on the river, other than the splash of the oars, were from nature's chorus – frogs and birds mainly, and the wind through the trees. [3]

Further downstream, Lewis arrived at Marietta. Founded in 1788, it was the oldest settlement on the western side of the Ohio River, in what would later become the state of Ohio – a testament to the ferocity of the Wyandot Indians. Places like Wheeling and Holliday's Cove, upstream on the Virginia side, had been settled 15 years earlier – a like testament to the equal ferocity and stubbornness of the settlers of the Upper Ohio Valley.

The face of North America was changing as the frontier settlers pushed westward, using the same basic forting techniques to protect them as had worked so successfully in the Ohio Valley. Like the relentless pounding of an axe against a tree, the wilderness would soon be broken.

ABOUT THE AUTHOR

Michael Edward Nogay received his B.A. degree, *magna cum laude*, from West Virginia University in 1980, where he was elected to Phi Beta Kappa and served as editor of the *Daily Athenaeum*. He earned his law degree from Washington & Lee University in Lexington, Virginia. In 2009 he was selected for inclusion in *Virginia and West Virginia Super Lawyers*.

Mr. Nogay developed a lifelong love of West Virginia history from his father, the late Edward Nogay, who was a schoolteacher, retired Army officer, and Hancock County Commissioner. He dedicates this book to his mother, Theresa Gromek Nogay, in gratitude for her steady guidance.

Mr. Nogay resides near Weirton, West Virginia, with his wife Robin and their three children, Edward, Jennifer and Maximillian. He is a full-time trial lawyer and a part-time history writer and high school wrestling coach.

The chapter entitled "Holliday's Cove Fort" was previously published as a limited edition booklet to raise funds for the non-profit Weirton Area Museum in 2008.

Special thanks to the author's sister, Prof. Deborah Nogay Campbell, for proofreading; to Mrs. Diane Kopa for typing; to Mr. Dennis Jones for map graphics; to Mr. John Buxton for the incredible front cover artwork; and to Richard Pflug and Jane Melville of Tri-State Publishing, who never frowned at my repeated changes.

Last, but certainly not least, how can I thank Edward Nogay II, named after his grandfather, and proof that the trait of patience skips a generation? Without Eddie, this book would still be just an idea on his laptop computer, which he loaned me and showed me how to operate.

ENDNOTES

INTRODUCTION: AN UNBROKEN WILDERNESS

1. J.H. Newton, *History of the Pan-Handle* (Wheeling: 1879) 332.

2. Randolph C. Downes, *Council Fires on the Upper Ohio* (University of Pittsburgh Press: 1940) 18.

3. Downes, 18-19; Walter S. Dunn, Jr., *Choosing Sides on the Frontier in the American Revolution* (Praeger Publishing: 2007) 61-62.

4. Downes, 159.

5. Downes, 183.

6. Downes, 197-198.

7. Wills DeHass, *History of the Early Settlement and Indian Wars of Western Virginia* (Wheeling: 1851) 98.

8. James B. Whisker, *Arms Makers of Colonial America* (Susquehanna University Press: 1992) 21.

9. Dunn, 5 and 74.

10. R. Douglas Hurt, *The Ohio Frontier* (Indiana University Press: 1996) 29-32; George Laycock, *The Mountain Men* (Lyons Press: 1988) 18; Dunn, 64-65.

11. R.G. Thwaites, *The Revolution on the Upper Ohio, 1775-1777* (Wisconsin: 1908) 251, fn. 97.

12. R.G. Thwaites and L.P. Kellogg, *Frontier Defense on the Upper Ohio, 1777-1778* (Madison, WI: 1912) 45.

13. R.G. Thwaites, *The Revolution on the Upper Ohio, 1775-1777* (Wisconsin: 1908) 250.

CHAPTER I: CAPTAIN SAMUEL MASON: THE CRIMINAL COMMANDER

1. Boyd Crumrine, editor, *Minute Book of Virginia Court Held for Ohio County,* 14. (copy available at Schiappa Public Library, Steubenville, Ohio)

2. Brant & Fuller, *History of the Upper Ohio Valley, vol. I* "Illustrated" (Madison, WI: 1890) 62-63.

3. A.S. Withers, *Chronicles of Border Warfare* (Cincinnati: 1895; new edition) 221-223.

4. Crumrine, 25.

5. Jared C. Lobdell, *Further Materials on Lewis Wetzel and the Upper Ohio Frontier* (Heritage Books: 2005) 3.

6. Otto A. Rothert, *The Outlaws of Cave-in-Rock* (Cleveland: 1924; reprinted 1996) 164-165.

7. Mark Moran, et al, *Weird Illinois* (Sterling Publishing: 2005) 42-43.

8. Rothert, 169-172.

9. Moran, 42-43.

10. Rothert, 179-190.

11. Rothert, 199; 241-266.

CHAPTER II: THE MURDERS AT BAKER'S TAVERN

1. Comment by R.G. Thwaites to the revised edition of A.S. Withers' *Chronicles of Border Warfare* (Clarksburg: 1831) 149 (published 64 years later).

2. R.G. Thwaites and L.P. Kellogg, *Documentary History of Dunmore's War 1774* (Madison, WI: 1905), 9-17 (citing Draper Manuscripts, vol. 2S, page 34).

3. *Ibid.* 16

4. *Ibid.* 11-12

5. *Ibid.* 15

6. J.A. Caldwell, *History of Belmont and Jefferson Counties, Ohio* (Wheeling: 1880) 70

7. Caldwell, 73

8. Brant & Fuller, *History of the Upper Ohio Valley, Vol. 1* (Madison: 1891) 44

9. Anthony F.C. Wallace, *Jefferson and the Indians* (Harvard University Press: 2000)

10. Caldwell, 75

11. Caldwell, 77

12. Caldwell, 78

13. Caldwell, 79

14. Alan W. Eckert, *That Dark and Bloody River* (Bantam Books: 1995)

15. Eckert, 95

16. Meredith Mason Brown, *Frontiersman* (Baton Rouge: 2008) 189

17. Eckert, 105

18. Eckert, 541

CHAPTER III "FORTING UP"

1. Joseph Doddridge, *Notes on the Settlement and Indian Wars* (Wellsburg: 1824) 95.

2. Doddridge, 123.

3. R. Douglas Hurt, *The Ohio Frontier* (Indiana University Press: 1996) 284-285.

4. Elizabeth A. Perkins, *Border Life* (University of North Carolina Press: 1998) 22-23.

5. *Ibid. 32-33.*

6. J.A. Caldwell, *History of Belmont and Jefferson Counties, Ohio* (Wheeling: 1880) 61; Nancy L. Caldwell, *A History of Brooke County* (Wellsburg: 1975) 10.

7. Mary S. Ferguson, *The History of Holliday's Cove* (Weirton: 1976), 16-17; 23.

8. Edgar W. Hassler, *Old Westmoreland* (J.R. Weldin & Co.: 1900) 176.

9. McCulloch's Leap and his subsequent death at the hands of Indians is described by Peter Boyd in his *History of the Northern West Virginia Panhandle* (Wheeling: 1927) 94-100.

10. Boyd Crumrine, editor, *Minute Book of the Virginia Court Held for Ohio County* (no publication date given) 14, 25 and 78. (Copy available at Schiappa Public Library, Steubenville, Ohio)

11. Doddridge, 110.

12. Peter Boyd, *History of the Northern West Virginia Panhandle, Vol. I* (Wheeling: 1927) 238.

13. Otto A. Rothert, *The Outlaws of Cave-in-Rock* (Cleveland: 1924; republished 1996) 38-39.

14. Hurt, 254.

15. Hurt, 255-257.

CHAPTER IV: THE PUBLIC FORTS

1. Lois A. Fundis, Reference Librarian, Mary H. Weir Public Library, *A Short History of the Weirton Area*, available at www.weirton.lib. wv.us. See also, Mary Ferguson, *The History of Holliday's Cove*, *Weirton Daily Times*, December 21, 1973, 4 and December 15, 1973, 4. Susan Kearns, "Greathouse, Holliday First Settlers in 1700's," *Weirton Daily Times*, March 16, 1973, 25.

2. A.B. Brooks, *Story of Ft. Henry*, West Virginia History, Vol. I, No. 2, January 1940, pp. 110-118 (Published by West Virginia Archives and History); Louise Phelps Kellogg, Editor, *Frontier Advance on the Upper Ohio, 1778-1779* (Wisconsin Historical Society: 1916) 303, fn 2.

3. A.S. Withers, *Chronicles of Border Warfare* (Cincinnati: 1895), 226.

4. *Story of Ft. Henry*, ibid.; Wills DeHass, *History of the Early Settlements and Indian Wars of Western Virginia* (Wheeling: 1851) 229-230; and Withers, 227. See also, J.G. Newton, editor, *History of the Pan-Handle* (Wheeling: 1879), 104.

5. Brant & Fuller, *History of the Upper Ohio Valley* (Madison: 1891) 85-86. (In "illustrated" volume at page 67.)

6. & 7. Lucullus V. McWhorter, *The Border Settlers of Northwestern Virginia from 1768 to 1795* (Buckhannon, WV: 1915) 150-151. It should be noted that an 1834 investigation of Schoolcraft's claims by a pension agent questioned his accounts of his Revolutionary service, claiming he was too young to have served. His detailed affidavit, however, appears quite credible.

8. John C. Dann, editor (University of Chicago Press: 1999) 253-254.

9. T.L. Montgomery, editor, *Report on the Commission to Locate the Site of the Frontier Posts of Pennsylvania, vol. two* (Harrisburg: 1916) 490.

10. *Ibid.* at 345; Eckert, 271.

11. L.P. Kellogg, *Frontier Retreat on the Upper Ohio 1779-1781* (Wisconsin Historical Society: 1912), 119, 180 and 281.

12. L.P. Kellogg, *Frontier Advance on the Upper Ohio, 1778-1779* (Madison: 1916) 411

13. L.P. Kellogg, *Frontier Retreat on the Upper Ohio, 1779-1781*(Madison: 1917) 281

14. Alan W. Eckert, *That Dark and Bloody River* (Bantam Books: 1995) 273.

15. *Ibid.* 431. See also, J.G. Newton, editor, *History of the Pan-Handle* (Wheeling: 1879) 144.

16. Eckert, 258; 434-435. See also, William Hintzen, *The Heroic Age: Tales of Wheeling's Frontier Era* (Closson Press: 2000) 128.

17. Eckert, 197 and 446; Hintzen, 124-125.

18. L.P. Kellogg, editor, *Frontier Advance on the Upper Ohio, 1778-1779*, (Wisconsin Historical Society: 1916) 384.

19. See, www.ohiohistorycentral.org, a website maintained by the Ohio Historical Society. For further reading, see, Gary S. Williams, *The Forts of Ohio: a Guide to Military Stockades* (Buckeye Book Press: 2003).

20. John R. Holmes, *The Story of Fort Steuben* (Fort Steuben Press 2000) 39. Holmes refers to VanSwearingen as encamped in "Cox's Fort (present-day Weirton)" in 1786 but later corrects the location of the Cox Blockhouse to be in Wellsburg (page 85).

21. *Ibid.* 51.

22. Jack Welch, *History of Hancock County* (Wheeling: 1963) 28-29; Eckert, amplification note 768; J.H. Newton, *History of the Pan-Handle* (Wheeling; 1879) 317-319.

23. The Wyandot Indians controlled much of Ohio in the late 1700's. They were fierce warriors who defeated Col. William Crawford and his army in 1782 near Upper Sandusky. Col. Crawford was captured and burned at the stake. See, www.ohiohistorycentral.org and www.ohioweb.ohiohistory.org. Both websites are maintained by the Ohio Historical Society.

24. Eckert, 617.

25. J.H. Newton, *History of the Pan-Handle* (Wheeling: 1879) 95.

26. Zane Grey, *Betty Zane* (New York: 1903) 27.

27. Draper Manuscripts, vol. 25. J.H. Newton *History of the Pan-Handle* (Wheeling: 1879) 93.

28. See, R.S. Klein and A. H. Cooper, *The Fort Henry Story* (Ft. Henry Bicentennial Committee: 1982) (fort built with the help of 400 militia); C.A. Wingerter, *History of Greater Wheeling and Vicinity* (Chicago: 1912) (built by Captain Crawford and about 200 men from Ft. Dunmore); J.H. Newton, *History of the Pan-Handle* (Wheeling: 1879) (200 men from Ft. Pitt under the command of Captain Crawford built the fort); William Hintzen and Joseph Roxby, *The Tales of Wheeling's Heroic Age* (Closson Press: 2000) (these authors state that "a work force of nearly 400 men" constructed the fort).

29. Alan W. Eckert, *That Dark and Bloody River* (Bantam Books: 1995) 125.

30. Eckert, 120-141; Hintzen, 28-30.

31. Eckert, 137 and 141; Hintzen, 29.

32. Eckert, 141-147; Hintzen, 32-35.

33. Eckert, 143-147.

34. C.B. Allman, *The Life and Times of Lewis Wetzel* (1932; republished by Heritage Books: 2007) 46.

35. Newton, 109.

36. Newton, 111.

37. Newton, 125.

38. Newton, 127.

39. Lucullus v. McWhorter, *Border Settlers of Northwestern Virginia* (Buckhannon, WV: 1915) 155.

40. Klein and Cooper, 9.

41. Eckert, 273; Edgar W. Hassler, *Old Westmoreland* (J.R. Weldin & Co.: 1900) 125.

42. Eckert, 444 and 533-534.

CHAPTER V: THE "FAMILY" FORTS and BLOCKHOUSES

1. Ruth Henthorne, et al, *The History of Newell and Vicinity* (1982) 8-9.

2. Alan W. Eckert, *That Dark and Bloody River* (Bantam Books: 1995) 38 and 56.

3. Wills DeHass, *History of the Early Settlement and Indian Wars of Western Virginia* (Wheeling: 1851) 365-371; Alan W. Eckert, *That Dark and Bloody River* (Bantam: 1995) 284-288, 697; Joseph Doddridge, *Notes on the Settlement and Indian Wars* (Reprinted, Pittsburgh: 1912) 235; Jared C. Lobdell, *Further Materials on Lewis Wetzel and the Upper Ohio Frontier* (Heritage Books: 1995) 16-17; Edgar W. Hassler, *Old Westmoreland* (J.R. Weldin & Co.: 1900) 151-152.

4. Janet White and Dale Patterson, *Hancock County* (Privately published, 1996); "Old Stone Church Rich in History," *The (East Liverpool) Weekly Echo,* January 30, 1991, 6; Jean Milton, *Windows on Hancock County* (Newell: 2000) 36-37.

5. Eckert, 431.

6. Mary S. Ferguson, *History of Holliday's Cove* (Weirton, WV: 1976) 128; J. H. Newton, *History of the Pan-Handle* (Wheeling: 1879) 317-319; Alan W. Eckert, *That Dark and* Bloody *River* (Bantam: 1995) amplification note 768.

7. Eckert, 323

8. J.G. Jacob, *Brooke County Record* (Wellsburg: 1882) 165.

9. *Sims Index to Land Grants in West Virginia* (1952) 565.

10. Edward T. Heald, *The Founding of Steubenville, 1796-1802* (1948) 23-42

11. R.G. Thwaites, *Frontier Defense on the Upper Ohio, 1777-1778* (Madison, WI: 1912) 40, fn. 81.

12. L.P. Kellogg, *Frontier Retreat on the Upper Ohio, 1779-1781* (Madison, WI: 1917) 415.

13. John R. Holmes, *The Story of Fort Steuben* (Fort Steuben Press: 2000) 39 and 85

14. L.P. Kellogg, *Frontier Retreat on the Upper Ohio, 1779-1781* (Madison, WI: 1917) 415, fn. 2.

15. R.G. Thwaites and L.P. Kellogg, *The Revolution on the Upper Ohio, 1775-1777* (State Historical Society of Wisconsin: 1908) 243.

16. R.G. Thwaites, *Frontier Defense on the Upper Ohio, 1777-1778* (Madison: 1912) 36

17. R.G. Thwaites, *Frontier Defense on the Upper Ohio, 1777-1778* (Madison, WI: 1912) 56, 62-63; Wills DeHass, *History of the Early Settlement and Indian Wars of Western Virginia* (Wheeling: 1851) 229, fn.1.

18. R.G. Thwaites, *Frontier Defense on the Upper Ohio, 1777-1778* (Madison, WI: 1912) 134; see also, 130.

19. J.H. Newton, *History of the Pan-Handle* (Wheeling: 1879) 315.

20. R.G. Thwaites and L.P. Kellogg, *Frontier Defense on the Upper Ohio, 1777-1778* (Madison, WI: 1912) 61

21. L.P. Kellogg, *Frontier Retreat on the Upper Ohio, 1779-1781* (Madison, WI: 1917) 420; Eckert, 273.

22. Brant & Fuller, *History of the Upper Ohio Valley* (Madison, WI: 1891) 85-86.

23. A.S. Withers, *Chronicles of Border Warfare* (Cincinnati: 1895) 151.

24. A.S. Withers, 221, fn. 1; R.G. Thwaites, *Frontier Defense on the Upper Ohio, 1777-1778* (Madison, WI: 1912) 55.

25. L.P. Kellogg, *Frontier Retreat on the Upper Ohio, 1779-1781* (Madison, WI: 1917) 313, fn. 1.

26. *Ibid.* 322.

27. Peter Boyd, *History of the Northern West Virginia Panhandle* (Wheeling: 1927) 94-100.

28. Alan W. Eckert, *That Dark and Bloody River* (Bantam Books: 1995) 108-135; 141-146; R.G. Thwaites and L.P. Kellogg, *Frontier Defense on the Upper Ohio, 1777-1778* (Madison : 1912) 61, fn.18; See also, Hintzen & Roxby, *The Heroic Age* (Closson Press: 2000) 35-40. Hintzen indicates the site of the ambush was known as "McMechen's Narrows."

29. Thomas Montgomery, *The Commission to Locate the Frontier Forts of Pennsylvania, Vol. II* (Harrisburg: 1916) 426 (hereinafter "Montgomery"); DeMay, 140-141.

30. Montgomery, 416-418; Doddridge, 200-201; John A. DeMay, *The Settlers' Forts of Western Pennsylvania* (Closson Press: 1997) 142-143 (hereinafter DeMay).

31. Montgomery, 404-410; Doddridge, 217; DeMay 171-173 (drawings at 176-177).

32. Eckert, 211-213; 237-238; 253; 329; DeMay, 133.

33. Eckert, 329; Montgomery, 414-415. But see, Scott Powell, *History of Marshall County* (Moundsville: 1925) 45.

34. Montgomery, 415-416; DeMay 137-139.

35. Montgomery, 423-424; DeMay, 192-193.

36. Montgomery, 432-433.

37. Montgomery, 421-423.

38. Montgomery, 418; Dann, 254.

39. Montgomery, 429.

40. Joseph Doddridge, *Notes on the Settlement and Indian Wars* (Reprinted, Pittsburgh: 1912) 235, fn.1.

41. Kenneth P. Bailey, *The Ohio Company of Virginia* (Glendale, CA: 1939) 125-140.

42. Montgomery, 442-443 ; Eckert, 243.

CHAPTER VI: CONTINENTAL AND MILITIA TROOPS (1775-1788)

1. Lucullus V. McWhorter, *Border Settlers of Northwestern Virginia* (Buckhannon, WV: 1915) 455.

2. R.G. Thwaites and L.P. Kellogg, *The Revolution on the Upper Ohio, 1775-1777* (Madison, WI: 1908) 13, 18-19 and 23, fn. 47.

3. R.G. Thwaites and L.P. Kellogg, *Frontier Defense on the Upper Ohio, 1777-1778* (Madison, WI: 1912) 293-294.

CHAPTER VII: THE STORY OF JOHN STRUTHERS

This chapter is based upon the revolutionary war pension application of John Struthers as found in the National Archives and published by John C. Dann, editor.

1. John C. Dann, editor, *The Revolution Remembered: Eyewitness Accounts of the War for Independence* (Univ. of Chicago Press: 1980)

CHAPTER VIII: SIMON GIRTY

1. "Descendant Makes a Case for Simon Girty," Pittsburgh *Post-Gazette*, Dec. 29, 1999; J.H. Newton, *History of the Pan-Handle* (Wheeling: 1879) 149.

2. R. Douglas Hunt, *The Ohio Frontier* (Indiana University Press: 1996) 29. L.P. Kellogg, *Frontier Retreat on the Upper Ohio, 1779-1781* (Madison, WI : 1917) 299, fn.1; R.G. Thwaites, *Frontier Defense on the Upper Ohio, 1777-1778* (Madison, WI: 1912)234-235, fn.98.

3. Lucullus V. McWhorter, *Border Settlers of Western Virginia* (Buckhannon, WV: 1915) 151.

4. Consul W. Butterfield, *A Historical Account of the Expedition Against Sandusky under Colonel William Crawford in 1782* (Cincinnati: 1873) 81-104; Edgar W. Hassler, *Old Westmoreland* (J.R. Weldin & Co.: 1900) 164.

5. Daniel P. Barr, "A Monster So Brutal," *Essays in History, vol. 40* (University of Virginia: 1998).

6. Phillip W. Hoffman, *Simon Girty, Turncoat Hero* (Flying Camp Press: 2003) 3.

7. Edna Kenton, *Simon Kenton (*New York: 1930) 120-122, as quoted by Phillip W. Hoffman, *Simon Girty, Turncoat Hero* (Flying Camp Press: 2003) 112-114.

8. L.P. Kellogg, *Frontier Advance on the Upper Ohio, 1778-1779* (Madison, WI: 1916) 384.

9. Hoffman, 171-176.

10. J.A. Caldwell, *History of Belmont and Jefferson Counties, Ohio* (Wheeling: 1880)147-149; Eckert, 570.

11. Hoffman, 268-286.

CHAPTER IX: BIG JOHN WETZEL'S SONS

1. C.B. Allman, *Life and Times of Lewis Wetzel* (1931; reprinted by Heritage Books: 2007) 3.

2. Jared C. Lodbell, *Further Materials on Lewis Wetzel and the Upper Ohio Valley* (Heritage Books: 2005) 14-15; Alan W. Eckert, *That Dark and Bloody River* (Bantam Books: 1995) 331-333.

3. J.H. Newton, *History of the Pan-Handle* (Wheeling: 1879) 136-137.

4. Alan W. Eckert, *That Dark and Bloody River* (Bantam: 1995) 256, 456, 476, and 633.

5. Gayle Thornbrough, editor, *Outpost on the Wabash* (Indianapolis: 1957) 208, as cited by George Carroll, *Lewis Wetzel: Warfare Tactics on the Frontier*, West Virginia Division of Culture and History, vol. 50, pp. 79-80 (1991).

6. Newton, 137-140.

7. Allman, 176.

8. George Carroll, *Lewis Wetzel: Warfare Tactics on the Frontier*, West Virginia Division of Culture and History, vol. 50, pp. 79-90 (1991), citing Draper MSS, 6E39 and Draper MSS 11E132.

9. *Ibid.*

10. Newton, 140-141; Gary S. Williams, *Spies, Scoundrels and Rogues on the Ohio Frontier* (Buckeye Book Press: 2005) 98; Carroll, fn. 15.

11. Alan W. Eckert, *That Dark and Bloody River* (Bantam: 1995) 753.

CHAPTER X : THE PENNSYLVANIA RIFLE AND OTHER FRONTIER WEAPONRY

1. Michael Edward Nogay, "Early Fly Fishing with the Kentucky Reel," *The American Fly Fisher* (Journal of the American Museum of Fly Fishing), Summer 1992, vol. 18 no.3; See also, Steven K. Vernon and Frank M. Stewart, *Fishing Reel Makers of Kentucky* (Plano, TX: 1992).

2. For a concise discussion of flintlock and percussion locks, see www.coon-n-crockett.org; Henry J. Kauffman, *The Pennsylvania-Kentucky Rifle* (New York: 1960).

3. Alan W. Eckert, *That Dark and Bloody River* (Bantam: 1995) 585-590.

4. James B. Whisker, *Arms Makers of Colonial America* (Susquehanna University Press: 1992) 21-22.

5. George Carroll, "Lewis Wetzel: Warfare Tactics on the Frontier," West Virginia Division of Culture and History, vol.51 (1991), quoting from James Buchanan, "Sketches of the History, Manners and Customs of the North American Indians," *The London Quarterly Review* 61 (1824) 102-103.

6. Joseph Doddridge, *Notes on the Settlement and Indian Wars* (Wellsburg: 1824) 123.

7. *Ibid.* 104.

8. Draper MSS 7E58, cited by George Carroll, *Lewis Wetzel: Warfare Tactics on the Frontier,* West Virginia Division of Culture and History, vol. 50, pp. 79-90 (1991).

9. Doddridge, 122.

CONCLUSION: A WILDERNESS BROKEN

1. Elizabeth A. Perkins, *Border Life* (University of North Carolina Press: 1998) 47.

2. Stephen E. Ambrose, *Undaunted Courage* (Simon & Shuster: 1996) 111.

3. Ambrose, 112.